UNLOCK

Second Edition

4

Reading, Writing & Critical Thinking

STUDENT'S BOOK WITH DIGITAL PACK

Chris Sowton and Alan S. Kennedy
with Jessica Williams, Christina Cavage
and Anita Sunda

CAMBRIDGE
UNIVERSITY PRESS

CAMBRIDGE
UNIVERSITY PRESS

University Printing House, Cambridge CB2 8BS, United Kingdom

One Liberty Plaza, 20th Floor, New York, NY 10006, USA

477 Williamstown Road, Port Melbourne, VIC 3207, Australia

314–321, 3rd Floor, Plot 3, Splendor Forum, Jasola District Centre, New Delhi – 110025, India

103 Penang Road, #05-06/07, Visioncrest Commercial, Singapore 238467

Cambridge University Press is part of the University of Cambridge.

It furthers the University's mission by disseminating knowledge in the pursuit of education, learning and research at the highest international levels of excellence.

www.cambridge.org
Information on this title: www.cambridge.org/9781009031417

First published 2014
Second Edition 2019
Second Edition update published 2021

20 19 18 17 16 15 14 13 12 11 10 9 8

Printed in Malaysia by Vivar Printing

A catalogue record for this publication is available from the British Library

ISBN 978-1-009-03141-7 Reading, Writing and Critical Thinking Student's Book with Digital Pack 4
ISBN 978-1-009-03131-8 Reading, Writing and Critical Thinking Student's eBook with Digital Pack 4

CONTENTS

MAP OF THE BOOK

UNIT	VIDEO	READING	VOCABULARY
1 GLOBALIZATION Reading 1: IKEA's global success (Business) Reading 2: Changing eating habits in Italy (Economics / Cultural studies)	China plans revival of Silk Road trade routes	***Key reading skill:*** Making predictions from a text type Topic sentences ***Additional skills:*** Understanding key vocabulary Using your knowledge Reading for main ideas Reading for detail Making inferences Identifying purpose and audience Synthesizing	Academic alternatives to phrasal verbs Globalization vocabulary
2 EDUCATION Reading 1: University courses: Business vs Engineering (Education / Sociology) Reading 2: Distance learning vs face-to-face learning (Education)	Disadvantaged children take part in trial of private tutor app	***Key reading skill:*** Making inferences ***Additional skills:*** Understanding key vocabulary Using your knowledge Reading for main ideas Reading for detail Synthesizing	Education vocabulary Academic words
3 MEDICINE Reading 1: The homeopathy debate (Medical ethics) Reading 2: Should healthcare be free? (Economics)	Robot revolution: robotic surgery is on the rise	***Key reading skill:*** Annotating a text ***Additional skills:*** Understanding key vocabulary Using your knowledge Skimming Reading for main ideas Reading for detail Identifying opinions Scanning to find key words Making inferences Synthesizing	Medical vocabulary Academic vocabulary
4 THE ENVIRONMENT Reading 1: Disaster mitigation (Meteorology) Reading 2: Combatting drought in rural Africa (Environment)	Population and water	***Key reading skill:*** Identifying cohesive devices ***Additional skills:*** Understanding key vocabulary Using your knowledge Predicting content using visuals Skimming Reading for main ideas Reading for detail Making inferences Synthesizing	Academic noun phrases Natural disaster vocabulary

	GRAMMAR	CRITICAL THINKING	WRITING
	Grammar for writing: Noun phrases Time phrases	Evaluating supporting examples Using tables and diagrams	***Academic writing skills:*** Essay structure Writing an effective thesis statement ***Writing task type:*** Write an explanatory essay ***Writing task:*** How has globalization changed your country?
	Grammar for writing: Comparison and contrast language: • Transitions to show comparison and contrast • Adverb clauses of contrast	Analyzing similarities and differences Using a Venn diagram	***Academic writing skills:*** Avoiding run-on sentences and comma splices Comparison and contrast essays ***Writing task type:*** Write a comparison and contrast essay ***Writing task:*** Discuss the similarities and differences between studying a language and studying Mathematics.
	Grammar for writing: Articles Transitions to show concession	Evaluating ideas	***Academic writing skill:*** Sentence variety ***Writing task type:*** Write an opinion essay ***Writing task:*** Is disease prevention the responsibility of individuals and their families, or of the government?
	Grammar for writing: Expressing solutions using *it*	Analyzing a case study Evaluating arguments	***Academic writing skills:*** Developing ideas Parallel structure ***Writing task type:*** Write a problem-solution essay ***Writing task:*** Write an essay which provides both short- and long-term solutions to an environmental problem and takes the costs into consideration. Refer to a specific case study in your essay.

UNIT	VIDEO	READING	VOCABULARY
5 ARCHITECTURE Reading 1: We need more green buildings (Environmental planning) Reading 2: Building design: form vs function (Building design)	Government grants for warmer, cheaper housing	***Key reading skill:*** Skimming a text ***Additional skills:*** Understanding key vocabulary Using your knowledge Reading for detail Summarizing Understanding paraphrase Making inferences Synthesizing	Academic word families Architecture and planning vocabulary
6 ENERGY Reading 1: Alternative energy (Energy development) Reading 2: Maintaining our vital natural resources (Environment)	The power of the wind	***Key reading skill:*** Working out meaning from context ***Additional skills:*** Understanding key vocabulary Using your knowledge Predicting content using visuals Reading for main ideas Reading for detail Making inferences Synthesizing	Energy collocations Formal and informal academic verbs
7 ART AND DESIGN Reading 1: All that art is (Fine art) Reading 2: Photography as art (Photography)	Beijing Art Zone	***Key reading skill:*** Scanning to find information ***Additional skills:*** Understanding key vocabulary Using your knowledge Predicting content using visuals Reading for detail Making inferences Understanding paraphrase Synthesizing	Vocabulary for art and design
8 AGEING Reading 1: The social and economic impact of ageing (Economics) Reading 2: What are the impacts of a young population on a society? (Social anthropology)	The retired men and women who love to walk	***Key reading skill:*** Identifying evidence in a text ***Additional skills:*** Understanding key vocabulary Using your knowledge Reading for main ideas Reading for detail Working out meaning Synthesizing	Academic collocations with prepositions

GRAMMAR	CRITICAL THINKING	WRITING
Grammar for writing: Register in academic writing	Creating a persuasive argument	***Academic writing skills:*** Ordering information Prioritizing arguments ***Writing task type:*** Write a persuasive essay ***Writing task:*** Which is more important when building or buying a new home: its location or its size?
Grammar for writing: Relative clauses	Evaluating benefits and drawbacks Organizing ideas for an essay	***Academic writing skills:*** Introducing advantages and disadvantages Coherence ***Writing task type:*** Write an advantages and disadvantages essay ***Writing task:*** Explain the advantages and disadvantages of three types of renewable energy and decide which would work best in your country.
Paraphrasing quotations ***Grammar for writing:*** Substitution Ellipsis	Understanding and evaluating analogies	***Academic writing skills:*** Arguments, counter-arguments and refutations ***Writing task type:*** Write an argumentative essay ***Writing task:*** Fashion, cooking and video games have all been likened to fine art. Choose *one* of these and discuss whether it should be considered fine art, comparable to painting or sculpture.
Cause and effect ***Grammar for writing:*** Language of prediction The first conditional	Drawing appropriate conclusions from graphical data	***Academic writing skills:*** Numerical words and phrases Interpreting graphs and charts ***Writing task type:*** Write an analysis essay ***Writing task:*** Describe population trends in Japan. Use the data from the graph to support your claims. Suggest the potential impact on the country if the 2050 projections are correct.

YOUR GUIDE TO UNLOCK

Unlock your academic potential

Unlock Second Edition is a six-level, academic-light English course created to build the skills and language students need for their studies (CEFR Pre-A1 to C1). It develops students' ability to think critically in an academic context right from the start of their language learning. Every level has 100% new inspiring video on a range of academic topics.

Confidence in teaching.

Joy in learning.

Better Learning WITH UNLOCK SECOND EDITION

Better Learning is our simple approach where insights we've gained from research have helped shape content that drives results. We've listened to teachers all around the world and made changes so that *Unlock* Second Edition better supports students along the way to academic success.

CRITICAL THINKING

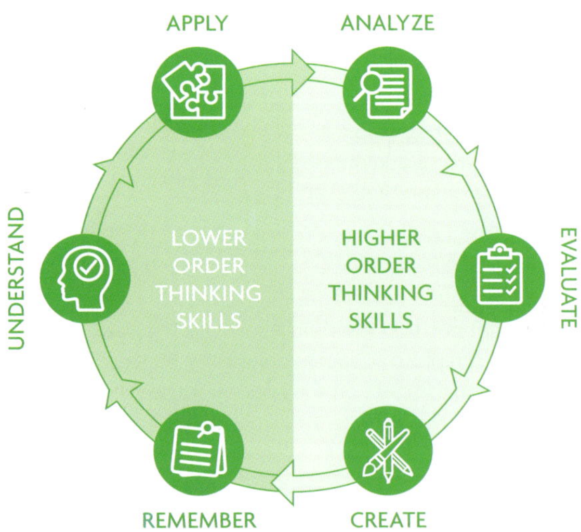

Critical thinking in *Unlock* Second Edition ...

- is **informed** by a range of academic research from Bloom in the 1950s, to Krathwohl and Anderson in the 2000s, to more recent considerations relating to 21st Century Skills
- has a **refined** syllabus with a better mix of higher- and lower-order critical thinking skills
- is **measurable**, with objectives and self-evaluation so students can track their critical thinking progress
- is **transparent** so teachers and students know when and why they're developing critical thinking skills
- is **supported** with professional development material for teachers so teachers can teach with confidence

... so that students have the best possible chance of academic success.

INSIGHT

Most classroom time is currently spent on developing lower-order critical thinking skills. Students need to be able to use higher-order critical thinking skills too.

CONTENT

Unlock Second Edition includes the right mix of lower- and higher-order thinking skills development in every unit, with clear learning objectives.

RESULTS

Students are better prepared for their academic studies and have the confidence to apply the critical thinking skills they have developed.

DIGITAL CLASSROOM MATERIAL

The *Unlock* Second Edition Digital Classroom Material ...

- offers extra, **motivating** practice in speaking, critical thinking and language
- provides a **convenient** bank of language and skills reference informed by our exclusive Corpus research
- is easily **accessible** and **navigable** from students' mobile phones
- is fully **integrated** into every unit
- provides Unlock-**specific** activities to extend the lesson whenever you see this symbol

... so that students can easily get the right, extra practice they need, when they need it.

INSIGHT

The digital classroom material is most effective when it's an integral, well-timed part of a lesson.

CONTENT

Every unit of *Unlock* Second Edition is enhanced with bespoke digital classroom material to extend the skills and language students are learning in the book. The symbol shows when to use the material.

RESULTS

Students are motivated by having relevant extension material on their mobile phones to maximize their language learning. Teachers are reassured that the material adds real language-learning value to their lessons.

RESEARCH

We have gained deeper insights to inform *Unlock* Second Edition by ...

- carrying out **extensive market research** with teachers and students to fully understand their needs throughout the course's development
- consulting **academic research** into critical thinking
- refining our vocabulary syllabus using our **exclusive Corpus research**

... so that you can be assured of the quality of *Unlock* Second Edition.

INSIGHT

- Consultation with global Advisory Panel
- Comprehensive reviews of material
- Face-to-face interviews and Skype™ calls
- Classroom observations

CONTENT

- Improved critical thinking
- 100% new video and video lessons
- Clearer contexts for language presentation and practice
- Text-by-text glossaries
- More supportive writing sections
- Digital workbook with more robust content
- Comprehensive teacher support

RESULTS

"Thank you for all the effort you've put into developing Unlock *Second Edition. As far as I can see, I think the new edition is more academic and more appealing to young adults."*

Burçin Gönülsen,
Işık Üniversity, Turkey

HOW *UNLOCK* WORKS

Unlock your knowledge

Encourages discussion around the themes of the unit with inspiration from interesting questions and striking images.

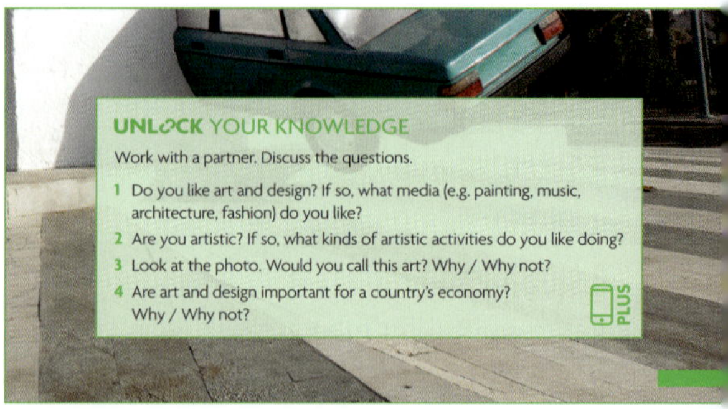

Watch and listen

Features an engaging and motivating video which generates interest in the topic and develops listening skills.

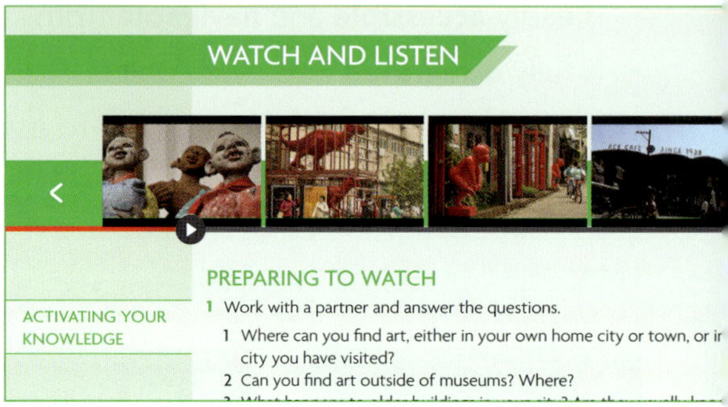

READING

Reading 1

The first text offers students the opportunity to develop the reading skills required to process academic texts, and presents and practises the vocabulary needed to comprehend the text itself.

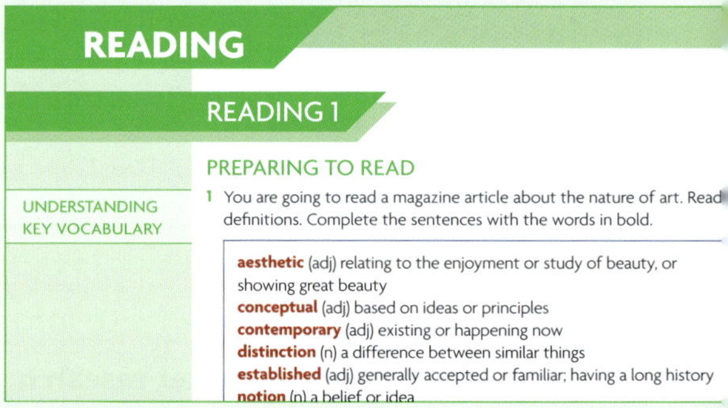

Reading 2

Presents a second text which provides a different angle on the topic and serves as a model text for the writing task.

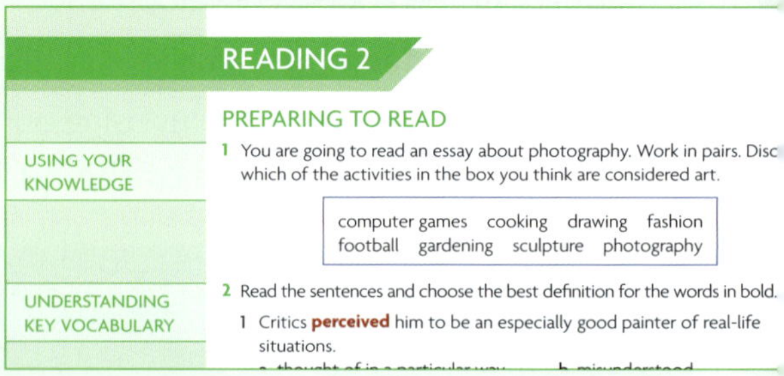

Language development

Consolidates and expands on the language presented in preparation for the writing task.

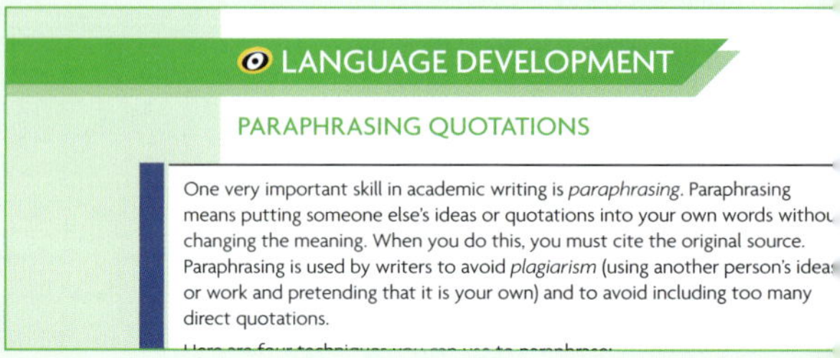

WRITING

Critical thinking

Develops the lower- and higher-order thinking skills required for the writing task.

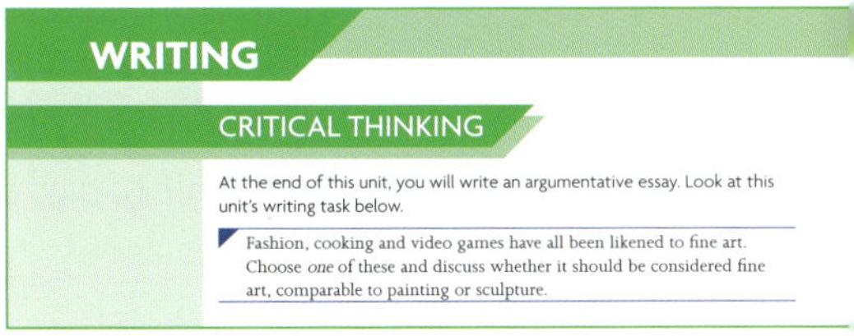
WRITING

CRITICAL THINKING

At the end of this unit, you will write an argumentative essay. Look at this unit's writing task below.

Fashion, cooking and video games have all been likened to fine art. Choose *one* of these and discuss whether it should be considered fine art, comparable to painting or sculpture.

Grammar for writing

Presents and practises grammatical structures and features needed for the writing task.

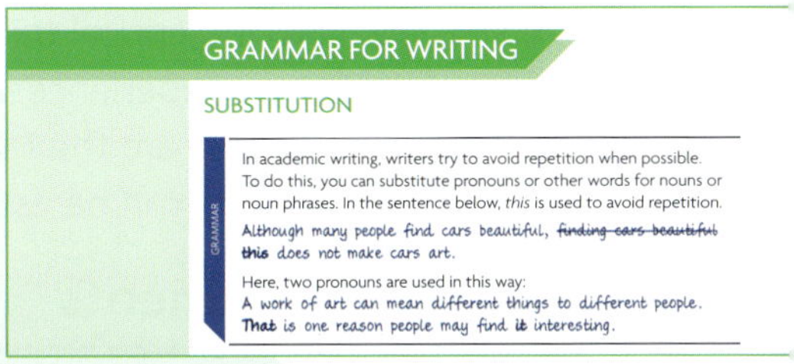
GRAMMAR FOR WRITING

SUBSTITUTION

GRAMMAR

In academic writing, writers try to avoid repetition when possible. To do this, you can substitute pronouns or other words for nouns or noun phrases. In the sentence below, *this* is used to avoid repetition.

Although many people find cars beautiful, ~~finding cars beautiful~~ **this** does not make cars art.

Here, two pronouns are used in this way:

A work of art can mean different things to different people.
That is one reason people may find **it** interesting.

Academic writing skills

Practises all the writing skills needed for the writing task.

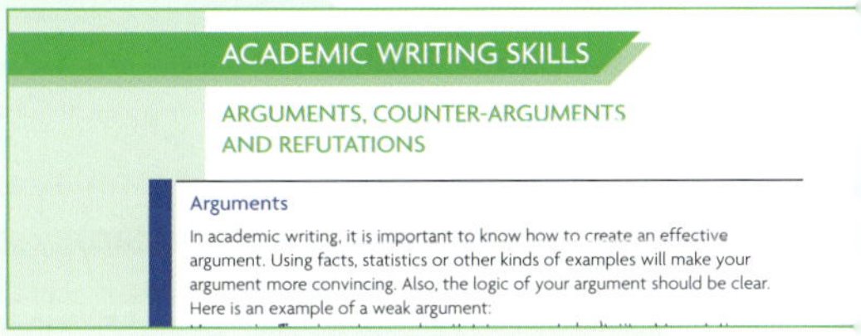
ACADEMIC WRITING SKILLS

ARGUMENTS, COUNTER-ARGUMENTS AND REFUTATIONS

Arguments

In academic writing, it is important to know how to create an effective argument. Using facts, statistics or other kinds of examples will make your argument more convincing. Also, the logic of your argument should be clear. Here is an example of a weak argument:

Writing task

Uses the skills and language learned throughout the unit to support students in drafting, producing and editing a piece of academic writing. This is the unit's main learning objective.

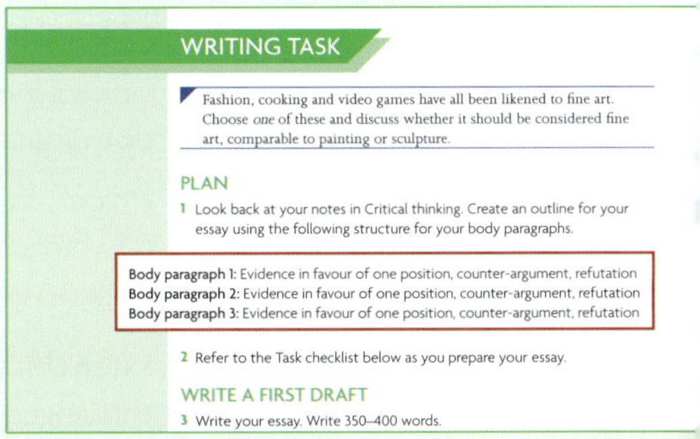
WRITING TASK

Fashion, cooking and video games have all been likened to fine art. Choose *one* of these and discuss whether it should be considered fine art, comparable to painting or sculpture.

PLAN

1 Look back at your notes in Critical thinking. Create an outline for your essay using the following structure for your body paragraphs.

Body paragraph 1: Evidence in favour of one position, counter-argument, refutation
Body paragraph 2: Evidence in favour of one position, counter-argument, refutation
Body paragraph 3: Evidence in favour of one position, counter-argument, refutation

2 Refer to the Task checklist below as you prepare your essay.

WRITE A FIRST DRAFT

3 Write your essay. Write 350–400 words.

Objectives review

Allows students to evaluate how well they have mastered the skills covered in the unit.

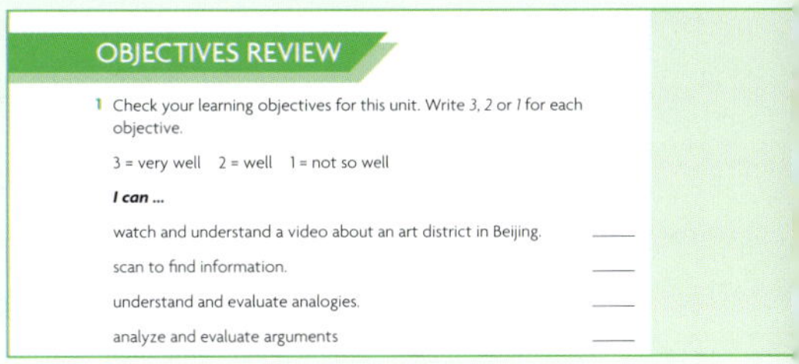
OBJECTIVES REVIEW

1 Check your learning objectives for this unit. Write *3*, *2* or *1* for each objective.

3 = very well 2 = well 1 = not so well

I can …

watch and understand a video about an art district in Beijing. ____

scan to find information. ____

understand and evaluate analogies. ____

analyze and evaluate arguments ____

Wordlist

Lists the key vocabulary from the unit. The most frequent words used at this level in an academic context are highlighted. ⊙

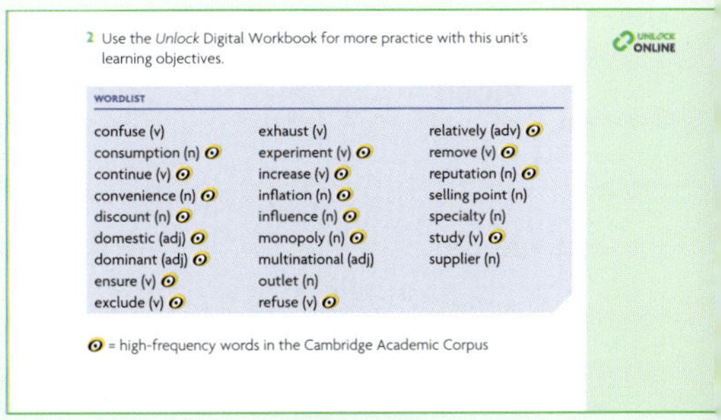
2 Use the *Unlock* Digital Workbook for more practice with this unit's learning objectives.

UNLOCK ONLINE

WORDLIST

confuse (v)	exhaust (v)	relatively (adv) ⊙
consumption (n) ⊙	experiment (v) ⊙	remove (v) ⊙
continue (v) ⊙	increase (v) ⊙	reputation (n) ⊙
convenience (n) ⊙	inflation (n) ⊙	selling point (n)
discount (n) ⊙	influence (n) ⊙	specialty (n)
domestic (adj) ⊙	monopoly (n) ⊙	study (v) ⊙
dominant (adj) ⊙	multinational (adj)	supplier (n)
ensure (v) ⊙	outlet (n)	
exclude (v) ⊙	refuse (v) ⊙	

⊙ = high-frequency words in the Cambridge Academic Corpus

COMPONENTS

Unlock offers 56 hours per Student's Book, which is extendable to 90 hours with the Digital Pack, and other additional activities in the Teacher's Manual and Development Pack.

Unlock is a paired-skills course with two separate Student's Books per level. For levels 1–5 (CEFR A1 – C1), these are ***Reading, Writing and Critical Thinking*** and ***Listening, Speaking and Critical Thinking***. They share the same unit topics so you have access to a wide range of material at each level. Each Student's Book provides access to the Digital Pack.

Unlock Basic has been developed for pre-A1 learners. ***Unlock Basic Skills*** integrates reading, writing, listening, speaking and critical thinking in one book to provide students with an effective and manageable learning experience. ***Unlock Basic Literacy*** develops and builds confidence in literacy. The *Basic* books also share the same unit topics and so can be used together or separately, and ***Unlock Basic Literacy*** can be used for self-study.

Student components

Resource	Description	Access
Student's Books	• Levels 1–5 come with the Digital Pack (Digital Workbook, Digital Classroom Material, downloadable audio and video) – Levels 1–4 (8 units) – Level 5 (10 units) • *Unlock Basic Skills* comes with downloadable audio and video (11 units) • *Unlock Basic Literacy* comes with downloadable audio (11 units)	• The Digital Pack (Digital Workbook, Digital Classroom Material, downloadable audio and video) is accessed on our **learning platform** via the unique code inside the front cover of the Student's Book • The audio and video are downloadable from the Student's Resources section on the **learning platform**
Digital Workbook	• Levels 1–5 only • Extension activities to further practise the language and skills learned • All-new vocabulary activities in the Digital Workbook practise the target vocabulary in new contexts	• The Digital Workbook is on our **learning platform** and is accessed via the unique code inside the front cover of the Student's Book
Digital Classroom Material	• Levels 1–5 only • Extra practice in speaking, critical thinking and language	• Please go to **cambridgeone.org** to access the digital classroom material. • Students use the same login details as for the **learning platform**, and then they are logged in for a year
Video	• Levels 1–5 and *Unlock Basic Skills* only • All the video from the course	• The video is downloadable from the Student's Resources section on the **learning platform**
Audio	• All the audio from the course	• The audio is downloadable from the Student's Resources section on the **learning platform**

Teacher components

Resource	Description	Access
Teacher's Manual and Development Pack	• One manual covers Levels 1–5 • It contains flexible lesson plans, lesson objectives, additional activities and common learner errors as well as professional development for teachers, *Developing critical thinking skills in your students* • It comes with downloadable audio and video, vocabulary worksheets and peer-to-peer teacher training worksheets	• The audio, video and worksheets are downloadable from the Teacher Resources section on the **learning platform**
Presentation Plus	• Software for interactive whiteboards so you can present the pages of the Student's Books and easily play audio and video, and check answers	• Presentation Plus is available from the Teacher Resources section on our **learning platform**

LEARNING OBJECTIVES	IN THIS UNIT YOU WILL …
Watch and listen	watch and understand a video about China's plans to revive the Silk Road trade routes.
Reading skills	make predictions from a text type; recognize topic sentences.
Critical thinking	evaluate supporting examples; use tables and diagrams.
Grammar	use noun phrases; use time phrases.
Academic writing skills	use correct essay structure; write an effective thesis statement.
Writing task	write an explanatory essay.

GLOBALIZATION

UNIT 1

UNLOCK YOUR KNOWLEDGE

Work with a partner. Discuss the questions.

1 Look at the photo. What types of products are made in your country and sold in others? Do you buy products from other countries?

2 Does it matter that people now import so many goods from other countries? Why / Why not?

3 What effects has globalization had on your country?

WATCH AND LISTEN

PREPARING TO WATCH

ACTIVATING YOUR KNOWLEDGE

1 You are going to watch a video about an important transport route. Before you watch, work with a partner and discuss the questions.

1. Where do most of the imported products in your country come from?
2. What products does your country export to other countries?
3. How are these products usually transported in and out of the country? Why?

PREDICTING CONTENT USING VISUALS

2 Work with a partner. Look at the pictures from the video and discuss the questions.

1. What kind of location is shown in the first picture? Where do you think it is?
2. What forms of transport do you see in the other pictures? What does it tell you about the location?
3. What do you think they are transporting? Where do you think they are coming from and going to?

GLOSSARY

the Silk Road (n) an ancient trade route from Asia to Europe, mainly across land

dry port (n) a transport centre where goods are loaded and unloaded, but which is not near water

logistics hub (n) a centre from which complicated activities are directed

infrastructure (n) the system of services in a country, including roads, bridges, power and water

think tank (n) a group of experts who work together to study a problem and suggest solutions

domestic (adj) related to issues inside a country

WHILE WATCHING

UNDERSTANDING MAIN IDEAS

3 Watch the video. Circle the sentence which best summarizes the main idea.

1 The Silk Road is an important part of China's history.
2 The Chinese government is aiming to create a giant trade network to connect Asia and Europe.
3 Korgas could be like other Chinese cities, such as Shenzhen and Shanghai.

UNDERSTANDING DETAIL

4 Watch again. Write *T* (true) or *F* (false) next to the statements below. Correct the false statements.

_____ 1 Korgas in China is the starting point of a new trading route.
____

_____ 2 Five years ago there was already lots of infrastructure in the area.
____

_____ 3 People in the area believe the project will be a success.
____

_____ 4 Building new roads and railways will help to create trade between countries.
____

_____ 5 The Chinese government's project only has economic goals.
____

WORKING OUT MEANING FROM CONTEXT

5 Work with a partner. Read the sentences from the video. What do you think the words and phrases in bold mean?

1 Five years ago, there was almost nothing here. All of this has been built **from scratch**.
2 Build the roads and rail links out into the regions' developing countries and the trade will follow, **so the theory goes**.
3 This is very much the image of the modern Silk Road the Chinese government wants to **project**.

DISCUSSION

6 Work with a partner and answer the questions.

1 Do you think international trade will increase or decrease in the future? Explain your answer.
2 What large infrastructure projects (a new airport, facilities for a large sporting event, etc.) have there been in your country recently? What impact have they had on the country?

READING

READING 1

PREPARING TO READ

UNDERSTANDING KEY VOCABULARY

1 Read the sentences and write the words in bold next to the definitions.

1 The countries with the strongest economies play the most **dominant** role in globalization.
2 My country experienced high **inflation** last year. Now things like food, housing and transport are much more expensive.
3 Nothing at that shop is sold at a **discount** – it's very expensive.
4 The shipping company has a **reputation** for thorough and on-time delivery. Customers have been very happy with their work.
5 Besides the excellent food at that restaurant, another **selling point** is the beautiful traditional Japanese art and furniture.
6 The corporation is a **multinational** organization with offices in Asia, Europe and Africa.
7 We can't repair the computers until our **supplier** sends us the special parts that we need to do it.
8 I usually buy fruit from local farmers to support the **domestic** economy.

a ____________ (adj) relating to a person's own country
b ____________ (adj) more important, strong, or noticeable than anything else of the same type
c ____________ (adj) a reduction in the usual price
d ____________ (n) the general opinion that people have about someone or something based on their behaviour or character in the past
e ____________ (n) a person or company that provides goods of a particular kind
f ____________ (n) a continuing rise in prices in an economy
g ____________ (adj) operating in different countries
h ____________ (n) a feature that persuades people to buy a product

SKILLS

Making predictions from a text type

Different text types, such as essays, articles and blogs, have different characteristics. Some will be more suitable for academic study than others. Before reading a text, you can make predictions about the information and the style of the writing. The source, title and any visuals can help you predict the content.

USING YOUR KNOWLEDGE

2 You are going to read a blog post. Before reading, which of the statements do you think will be true?

1 The style will be informal.
2 The contents will be appropriate for an academic essay.
3 The writer will give his or her personal opinions.
4 The information will be up-to-date.

3 Read the blog and check your predictions. Find examples to support your ideas.

IKEA'S GLOBAL SUCCESS

1 In this entry to my blog series about successful **multinational** companies, I will check out the furniture chain IKEA. IKEA has been the world's **dominant** furniture chain since 2008, according to *Forbes* magazine.

2 Swedish entrepreneur Ingvar Kamprad was only 17 years old when he started the company in 1943. These days, the chain has about 400 stores selling appliances[1], furniture and other household[2] items in over 40 countries around the world. So how have they managed to become such a global hit? Well, to me it seems that three features of the chain stand out: their dedication to research, their affordable prices and their eco-friendly[3] **reputation**.

3 The executives at IKEA have long understood the need to research other markets in order to succeed globally. The company is constantly conducting research on how people use their furniture and what they are looking for. They recently conducted research in eight cities worldwide. This is how they learned, for example, that Korean customers want a special *kimchi*[4] refrigerator.

4 But in order to sell at **discount** prices, they need to make and sell a lot of the same thing to keep costs low. This way, they can get low prices from **suppliers**, and charge super-low prices to their customers. As a result, they can keep their prices economical even during periods of **inflation**. This is why they will show the same products in different ways in their stores, depending on the local culture. A British bedroom display might have a British flag bedspread on it, whereas one in Tokyo may have a traditional mat on the floor. In China, IKEA's fastest-growing market, **domestic** manufacturers make most of the products they sell in order to keep transport costs low.

5 A final **selling point** for many customers is the image of the company. They sell their furniture in flat boxes which use less space and paper and are easier to transport. A company representative recently said that they are working on creating new products out of materials we currently throw away, such as recycled plastic and foil. In some markets, they plan to market an electric bicycle, and in Seoul, they recently planted a tree to celebrate the opening of a new store.

6 Next week, I'll look at other multinational companies which specialize in household goods and automobile production.

[1]**appliances** (n) a device, usually electrical, that is used in the home
[2]**household** (adj) related to people homes
[3]**eco-friendly** (adj) designed to do the least possible damage to the environment
[4]***kimchi*** (n) a traditional Korean vegetable dish

WHILE READING

READING FOR DETAIL

4 Answer the questions with information from the blog.

1 According to the introduction, why has the blogger written this blog entry about IKEA?

____

2 How might a display in a Japanese IKEA be different from one in the UK?

____

3 Why does the writer think that IKEA's shipping packaging is eco-friendly?

____

4 What does the writer plan to write about soon?

____

5 Read the blog again. Write *T* (true), *F* (false), or *DNS* (does not say) next to the statements. Correct the false statements.

1 IKEA's founder is from Sweden.

____

2 The author identifies three main characteristics of the chain which has made it globally successful.

____

3 The desire for IKEA executives to understand new markets is very recent.

____

4 IKEA has stores in China.

____

5 Some IKEA products use recycled glass.

____

6 IKEA has plans to sell electric bicycles in all markets where they operate.

____

6 The blog author uses some informal language. Match informal words and phrases to formal words. Use the context to help you.

1 check out	**a** a big success
2 super-low	**b** investigate
3 a hit	**c** very inexpensive

READING BETWEEN THE LINES

MAKING INFERENCES

7 Work with a partner. Discuss the questions.

1 What is the point of mentioning the *kimchi* refrigerator?
2 Why would eco-friendliness be a 'selling point' for some customers?
3 Do you think the author likes eco-friendly retailers? Why / Why not?

DISCUSSION

8 Work with a partner. Discuss the questions.

1 Do you read blogs or reviews online? Why / Why not? If you do, what are they usually about?
2 Have you ever written an online review? What was it for?
3 To what extent do online reviews influence whether or not you buy something?

READING 2

PREPARING TO READ

UNDERSTANDING KEY VOCABULARY

1 Read the definitions. Complete the sentences with the correct words in bold.

consumption (n) the amount of something that someone uses, eats or drinks
convenience (n) the state of being suitable for your purposes and causing the least difficulty
ensure (v) to make certain that something is done or happens
experiment (v) to test or to try a new way of doing something
increase (v) to become larger or greater
influence (n) the power to have an effect on people or things, or someone or something that is able to do this
relatively (adv) quite good, bad, etc. in comparison with other similar things or with what you expect
specialty (n) a product that a place is especially known for

1 Many shoppers have switched to ordering groceries online because of its ___________ . Now they don't leave their homes to buy food.
2 Others, however, prefer to see the food before they buy it to ___________ that the food is fresh.
3 People sometimes reduce their ___________ of certain foods when those foods become more expensive.
4 If bad weather affects the supply of some fruits or vegetables, it can cause their prices to ___________ .
5 People who live in big cities tend to be ___________ familiar with international food compared to people who live in rural areas.
6 In Iceland we tried a bread that is baked in the ground near a hot spring. It's a local ___________ .
7 Recently, the popularity of cooking programmes on television has had a big ___________ on the ingredients that people use. People want to cook with foods they see on TV.
8 Some travellers like to eat familiar food, but others prefer to ___________ with unfamiliar dishes.

PLUS

SKILLS

Topic sentences

Good paragraphs in formal writing usually start with *topic sentences*. These tell you the subject of the paragraph. After the topic sentence you can usually make a prediction about what information will follow. By reading the first sentence of each paragraph in a text, you can often identify which paragraph to look at if you need some specific information.

2 You are going to read an essay about changing eating habits in Italy. Read the topic sentences. Work with a partner and discuss what you think the rest of each paragraph will be about.

1 In Italy, changing trends have affected the preparation of food.
2 Italians' food tastes have changed because of globalization.
3 A third major change in Italy's food culture has been the rise of large restaurant chains.

3 Skim the essay and check your predictions from Exercise 2.

WHILE READING

READING FOR MAIN IDEAS

4 Read the essay. Do the topics in the table refer to the past, the present or both? Tick (✔) the correct column.

		past	present	both
1	mass production of pasta		✔	
2	making pasta sauce at home			
3	popularity of frozen food			
4	lack of foreign food in Italy			
5	the rise of large restaurant chains			
6	worldwide popularity of Italian food			

5 Complete the sentences with your own words.

1 Italian restaurants can be found ________________ .
2 In the past, it was not common for Italians to ________________ .
3 In Italian shops, you can now buy ________________ .
4 Although recent changes mean Italians have more time and more choice, some dislike the fact that local food is ________________ .

Changing eating habits in Italy

1 Globalization is causing a lot of change in international culture, from the TV shows we watch to the clothes we wear. One major area which has been affected by globalization is food culture. In a recent survey taken in Japan, Brazil and Canada, 72% of people said that globalization had improved their eating habits. It seems clear that globalization has significantly affected food **consumption** in most parts of the world, but one country whose food has a long history of being 'globalized' is Italy. If you walk down any main street in any major world city, you will find at least one Italian restaurant. Furthermore, Italy has seen changes in its own eating habits due to **influence** from other countries. This influence, which is a result of the broader trend of globalization, has had both advantages and disadvantages.

2 In Italy, changing trends have affected the preparation of food. Italian families have always taken a lot of pride in preparing food. Until recently, pasta – a basic Italian food – would have been made by people in their local area. Families would also have made the sauces to eat with the pasta at home. People no longer spend so much time preparing their meals. Indeed, frozen or take-out Italian meals have become very popular in Italy. Furthermore, dried pasta is now mass-produced[1] and is sold **relatively** cheaply in supermarkets. Ready-made pasta sauces are also increasingly popular – sales have doubled in the last five years, according to one manufacturer. This has added to the convenience of making meals, but has diminished[2] a cultural tradition.

3 Italians' food tastes have changed because of globalization. People are travelling more, being exposed to other cultures more, and reading about and seeing foreign ingredients and recipes on the internet and social media. Immigrants to Italy bring their food traditions with them. It used to be that people's opportunities to **experiment** with foreign food were very limited, since only pizza and pasta were available in the local town square. Now they can eat at restaurants with foreign cuisine[3] and buy foreign food in shops. Indian, Chinese and Japanese food have all become especially popular. While this trend is more common in urban areas such as Rome, Milan and Venice, many smaller towns are also experiencing similar changes. Many Italians would say that this has been a positive change, but others worry that they are losing their sense of nationality as foreign food becomes more common.

4 A third major change in Italy's food culture has been the rise of large restaurant chains. These chains are often foreign, and their numbers have **increased** enormously in recent years. Many people like the **convenience** of fast food. Some Italians, however, feel that this has resulted in the destruction of local and national **specialties**. In 1986, a famous fast-food chain opened a restaurant in a historic Rome neighbourhood. Many unhappy people responded by joining the 'Slow Food' movement. This movement encourages people to eat healthy, locally sourced food.

5 In summary, globalization has had a significant effect on the way that Italians eat. Its influence can be seen as both positive and negative. Convenience foods have replaced many of the traditional home-cooked meals, and the availability of foreign foods and international chains has greatly increased. Italians no longer have to rely on food which is produced locally. While some people welcome this extra choice, others fear the damage it may cause to Italian traditions, culture and local businesses. On the other hand, the great popularity of Italian food worldwide will **ensure** this great cuisine never disappears.

[1]**mass-produced** (adj) made in large amounts, using machinery in a factory
[2]**diminished** (v) made smaller; decreased
[3]**cuisine** (n) style of cooking

READING BETWEEN THE LINES

IDENTIFYING PURPOSE AND AUDIENCE

6 Work with a partner. Discuss the questions and choose the best answer.

1 What types of readers do you think this essay is meant to appeal to?
  a people who have a general interest in food
  b people who are experts in Italian food

2 What do you think is the author's main intention in writing this essay?
  a to say that globalization has had a largely positive impact on Italian food
  b to say that globalization has fundamentally changed Italian food

DISCUSSION

SYNTHESIZING

7 Work with a partner. Using ideas from Reading 1 and Reading 2, discuss the following questions.

1 Should governments limit the growth of multinational restaurant chains to allow local, traditional restaurants to compete for customers?
2 When you eat at a foreign food restaurant, which of these three qualities is most important to you: that it is *inexpensive*, that it is *locally owned* or that it is *authentic*? Why?

PLUS

LANGUAGE DEVELOPMENT

ACADEMIC ALTERNATIVES TO PHRASAL VERBS

VOCABULARY

When writing essays, it is important to use language which is more formal than you would use when speaking or writing informal pieces.

Phrasal verbs, which usually consist of a main verb followed by a particle (e.g., *up*, *on*), are less common in academic writing than in informal writing. In academic writing, phrasal verbs can often be replaced by a single word. Using these alternatives will make your writing more formal and academic.

1 Match the phrasal verbs to the academic verbs.

1 go on	**a** increase
2 go up	**b** continue
3 turn down	**c** study
4 look into	**d** confuse
5 use up	**e** remove
6 mix up	**f** refuse
7 leave out	**g** exclude
8 take away	**h** exhaust

2 Replace the phrasal verbs in bold with the correct form of the academic verbs from Exercise 1.

1 The amount of migrant labour is expected to **go up**. ___________
2 If multinational companies **go on** expanding, smaller local suppliers may die out. ___________
3 Academics have been **looking into** the implications of globalization for many years. ___________
4 Immigration can lead to people becoming **mixed up** about their sense of nationality. ___________
5 Although many people benefit from globalization, others can also be **left out**. ___________
6 Immigrants without suitable qualifications may have their visa requests **turned down**. ___________
7 When a country's natural resources are **used up**, they may need to rely on other countries to supply them. ___________
8 Some supporters of global economic freedom believe that all trade barriers should be **taken away**. ___________

PLUS

GLOBALIZATION VOCABULARY

3 Complete the text about globalization with words from the box. Use the Glossary on pages 190–191 to help you.

consumption	discounts	domestic	inflation
monopoly	multinational	outlets	

Customer buying habits have changed greatly in this age of globalization. Now, rather than just spending money on (1) ___________ products, people are interested in buying items from all over the world. In other words, globalization has changed patterns of (2) ___________ internationally. When certain chains become very popular worldwide, there is sometimes a fear that their local (3) ___________ in different countries will cause unfair competition. Large (4) ___________ companies which operate in many countries, such as IKEA or Starbucks, could start to have a (5) ___________ on the products they sell in foreign markets. The local companies are forced to compete with big retailers who can keep prices low. If the local companies can't match these (6) ___________, they will suffer financially. This is especially true in cases where there is (7) ___________ in a local economy which is causing the prices of many other things to rise.

PLUS

WRITING

CRITICAL THINKING

At the end of this unit, you are going to write an explanatory essay. Look at this unit's writing task below.

How has globalization changed your country?

SKILLS

Evaluating supporting examples

In academic writing, you need to justify and give supporting examples to any statements or opinions that you write to show that they are true. It is important to only use supporting examples which are relevant and appropriate for the point which you are making. In order to do this, you need to evaluate the examples properly.

APPLY

1 Read these statements. What examples are given in Reading 2 that can support them?

1 Italians pride themselves on the making and preparation of food.
2 People's opportunity to experiment with foreign food was very limited.
3 People no longer spend so much time preparing their meals.
4 Italians worry that they are losing their sense of nationality.
5 Globalization has become such a significant influence.

ANALYZE

2 Think of an aspect of globalization that you would like to write about in the Writing task. This can be about food, clothing, entertainment, holidays, language, technology or other aspects of globalization. Write this idea in the middle of the ideas map below, and add any supporting examples which you can think of.

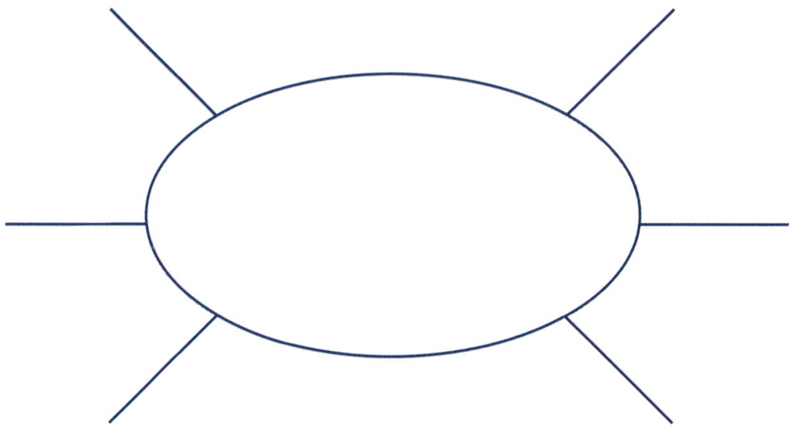

SKILLS

Using tables and diagrams

Tables and diagrams can often help you organize information that you can use to support your ideas in an essay.

CREATE

3 Complete the table below with the best three supporting examples from the ideas map in Exercise 2. It should follow the format of a body paragraph in an essay on the topic you chose in Exercise 2.

Topic:
Supporting example 1:
Supporting example 2:
Supporting example 3:
Concluding sentence:

GRAMMAR FOR WRITING

NOUN PHRASES

GRAMMAR

Noun phrases are two or more words which function as a noun in a sentence and contain one idea.

Noun phrases can be made by combining nouns with:

- other nouns: *technology companies*
- relative clauses: *a chain which is growing globally*
- prepositional phrases: *manufacturing in China*
- adjectives: *the dominant market*

In academic writing, many noun phrases are created by joining two nouns with *of*. These common phrases with *of* are used to talk about quantity: *a range of*.

1 Match the sets of noun phrases to grammar structures.

1 world cuisine
car factories
2 people in their local area
a fact of modern life
3 large chains
major city
4 a contribution that benefits us the most
a recent change which is unstoppable

a adjective + noun
b noun + prepositional phrase
c noun phrase + relative clause
d noun + noun

2 Rearrange the words to make noun phrases.

1 specialties / local
local specialties

2 range / a / exports / of

3 change / standards / in / environmental / a

4 of / exchange / ideas / the / technological

5 impact / chains / multinational / the / of

6 a / of / international / group / entrepreneurs

7 different / the / cultures / mixture / of

8 consumption / worldwide / an / in / increase

TIME PHRASES

GRAMMAR

In academic writing, it is helpful to use different phrases to describe the time in which something happened. You can also use these phrases to clarify whether events occurred in the past or are happening now. Sometimes you need to be specific. Other times, you can be more general.

Very specific: The refrigerated truck was invented **in 1939**.

More general: **In recent years**, foreign food has become more popular in Italy.

3 Put the time phrases below in the correct part of the table, according to the period of time they refer to.

around ten years ago at the present time
before the war currently formerly historically in recent years
in the 1990s in the eighteenth century in the past nowadays
presently these days

general past time	specific past time	present

4 Complete the sentences with information about food in your country.

1 Nowadays, you can buy ____ .

2 In recent years, my country has seen many new types of restaurants, such as ____ .

3 Until the 1990s, it was impossible to find ____ .

4 These days, there are many ____ .

5 Around ten years ago, you could not buy ____ .

6 Historically, people tended to live off ____ .

ACADEMIC WRITING SKILLS

ESSAY STRUCTURE

SKILLS

Although there are different types of academic essays, the overall structure and principles tend to be the same. Academic essays start with an *introductory paragraph*, followed by *body paragraphs* and end with a *concluding paragraph*.

Introductory paragraph

The first paragraph gets the reader's attention by beginning with a *hook* – an interesting fact or statement, a surprising statistic, a quotation or a question. For example, in Reading 2, a statistic based on a survey taken in Japan, Brazil and Canada ('72% of people said ...') grabs the reader's attention. Then the writer provides some background on the main topic of the essay. The paragraph ends with a *thesis statement*, which is the main idea of the essay and reflects the writer's point of view. In Reading 2, the thesis statement is:

This influence, which is a result of the broader trend of globalization, has had both advantages and disadvantages.

Body paragraphs

These develop the main ideas outlined in the introduction and include relevant evidence and supporting information.

Concluding paragraph

The last paragraph presents a restatement of the thesis of the essay and ends with the conclusions, recommendations or predictions of the writer.

1 Read the essay. Choose the best place (1–5) for each of the sentences (a–e).

(1) ______ Historians might suggest that it was when Christopher Columbus made his voyages to the Americas in the 1490s. For most of us, however, we tend to think of it as a more modern phenomenon connected with the rise of the worldwide web. In any case, when it comes to the question of whether globalization is beneficial or not, it is complicated. (2) ______ .

The international spread of information, technology, products and ideas has enriched our lives in many ways. When something new is invented far away, we can get it at home. Governments can share ideas with each other to keep us all safer. (3) ______ .

(4) ______ The increased movement of people across borders means that diseases can spread more quickly than before. Also, our economies are more linked, which means that when one country experiences a financial crisis, it can impact many others. Finally, large international corporations can create unfair competition for local businesses.

Clearly there are advantages and disadvantages to globalization. How to balance this is a debate that has been going on for some time. One thing seems clear, however: we citizens are more connected than ever before. (5) ______ .

- **a** When did globalization begin?
- **b** We can probably predict that this will not change.
- **c** However, there are also drawbacks.
- **d** A review of some of the features of globalization suggests that it has had both pros and cons.
- **e** Also, we can enjoy each others' cultures more than ever before by experiencing new food and different types of entertainment.

PLUS

WRITING AN EFFECTIVE THESIS STATEMENT

SKILLS

A thesis statement in an academic essay is usually found at the very end of the introductory paragraph. It explains what the entire essay will be about, and it expresses a writer's point of view. With a good thesis statement, readers can guess what the rest of the essay might look like.

A thesis statement should sound like an opinion. It should *not* sound like a fact, a question, a description of what the essay will contain, or a general idea which everyone agrees on.

Essay topic	Possible thesis statement
The effects of globalization	Globalization has brought us both advantages and disadvantages, but the benefits have been far greater than the drawbacks.
The global influence of the USA	It is a mistake to confuse globalization with Americanization.

Notice that in each case, you can imagine or guess what the rest of the essay might contain. None of these statements sound like facts, questions or descriptions of what will follow. Instead, they sound like points of view which the writer could argue.

2 Read the possible thesis statements. Decide if the statement would make a good thesis statement. If so, tick (✔) *OK*. If not, tick *F* (it sounds like a fact), *Q* (it is a question), *D* (it is a description of what the essay will contain) or *G* (it is an idea which is too general to work well as a thesis statement).

		OK	F	Q	D	G
1	Pasta dishes are very common in Italian cuisine.					
2	Should governments limit the number of chain restaurants?					
3	The exchange of cultures has been a huge benefit of globalization.					
4	Most people like to eat different kinds of food.					
5	Even though globalization is considered to be beneficial by many, it has actually done great harm to cultures around the world.					
6	I do not like broccoli, so I never eat it.					
7	The following essay will explain the drawbacks of globalization.					

International shops and restaurants in Chonburi, Thailand

3 Read the first sentences from an essay's introductory, body and concluding paragraphs. Then write an appropriate thesis statement in your own words that would make sense for this essay.

INTRO There is an ongoing discussion in economics about how globalization affects the developing countries of the world.
Thesis: ____

____

BODY 1 Large multinational companies from economically strong countries sometimes take advantage of the natural resources of a poorer country.
BODY 2 International companies operating in places where wages are generally low can pay local suppliers and workers less than they pay others.
CONCLUSION All this suggests that globalization has a harmful effect on certain countries.

4 Compare your thesis statement with a partner. Suggest changes if necessary.

WRITING TASK

How has globalization changed your country?

PLAN

1 In Reading 2 on page 23, each paragraph has a different function. Match each paragraph (1–5) to the functions below.

a Description of changes to food preparation ______
b Introduction ______
c Conclusion ______
d Description of changes to food tastes ______
e Description of changes to the restaurant industry ______

2 Look back at your notes from Exercises 2 and 3 in Critical thinking. Think of some other details about this aspect of globalization. Use your notes to help you plan your essay.

3 Decide the function of each paragraph in your essay. Write the functions in column A.

	A	B
paragraph 1		
paragraph 2		
paragraph 3		
paragraph 4		
paragraph 5		

4 Think about the supporting details and examples you are going to include in each paragraph. Write notes in column B.

5 Now think about a thesis statement that will work well for this essay. You can always go back and change it later if it does not match the rest of the essay.

6 Refer to the Task checklist on page 34 as you prepare your essay.

WRITE A FIRST DRAFT

7 Write the first draft of your essay. Use your essay plan to structure your essay. Include an introductory paragraph, a thesis statement, three body paragraphs with supporting ideas and a concluding paragraph with a final thought, recommendation or prediction. Write 350–400 words.

REVISE

8 Use the Task checklist to review your essay for content and structure.

TASK CHECKLIST	✔
Did you structure your essay?	
Does the introductory paragraph have a clear thesis statement?	
Does each paragraph focus on the information it is supposed to?	
Did you include topic sentences for each paragraph?	
Did you include evidence to support your topic sentences?	
Is there a concluding paragraph with a concluding thought, recommendation or prediction?	

9 Make any necessary changes to your essay.

EDIT

10 Use the Language checklist to edit your essay for language errors.

LANGUAGE CHECKLIST	✔
Do the words in any noun phrases appear in the right order?	
Did you use time phrases correctly?	
Did you use academic verbs instead of phrasal verbs where possible?	
Did you spell academic verbs correctly?	

11 Make any necessary changes to your essay.

OBJECTIVES REVIEW

1 Check your learning objectives for this unit. Write *3*, *2* or *1* for each objective.

3 = very well 2 = well 1 = not so well

I can ...

watch and understand a video about China's plans to revive the Silk Road trade routes.	_____
make predictions from a text type.	_____
recognize topic sentences.	_____
evaluate supporting examples.	_____
use tables and diagrams.	_____
use noun phrases.	_____
use time phrases.	_____
use correct essay structure.	_____
write an effective thesis statement.	_____
write an explanatory essay.	_____

2 Use the *Unlock* Digital Workbook for more practice with this unit's learning objectives.

UNLOCK ONLINE

WORDLIST

confuse (v)
consumption (n) ⊙
continue (v) ⊙
convenience (n) ⊙
discount (n) ⊙
domestic (adj) ⊙
dominant (adj) ⊙
ensure (v) ⊙
exclude (v) ⊙
exhaust (v)
experiment (v) ⊙
increase (v) ⊙
inflation (n) ⊙
influence (n) ⊙
monopoly (n) ⊙
multinational (adj)
outlet (n)
refuse (v) ⊙
relatively (adv) ⊙
remove (v) ⊙
reputation (n) ⊙
selling point (n)
specialty (n)
study (v) ⊙
supplier (n)

⊙ = high-frequency words in the Cambridge Academic Corpus

LEARNING OBJECTIVES	IN THIS UNIT YOU WILL ...
Watch and listen	watch and understand a video about an app that helps children catch up outside the classroom.
Reading skill	make inferences.
Critical thinking	analyze similarities and differences; use a Venn diagram to plan a comparison-contrast essay.
Grammar	use transitions to show comparison and contrast; use adverb clauses of contrast.
Academic writing skills	avoid run-on sentences and comma splices; write a comparison and contrast essay.
Writing task	write a comparison and contrast essay.

EDUCATION

UNIT 2

UNLOCK YOUR KNOWLEDGE

Work with a partner. Discuss the questions.

1. What exams do students in your country have to take?
2. Is there anything in your country's education system you would like to change? Why / Why not?
3. Look at the photo. What kind of technology are the students using? How can technology improve education?
4. Learning to do a specific skilled job, such as machine repair or farm work, is called *vocational training*. What are some advantages or disadvantages of vocational training over academic university study?

WATCH AND LISTEN

PREPARING TO WATCH

ACTIVATING YOUR KNOWLEDGE

1 Work with a partner and answer the questions.

1 Do some school pupils in your country get extra lessons from another teacher when they are not at school? When do you think they need extra tuition the most?
2 Do you think extra lessons are a good idea? Why / Why not?
3 Are extra lessons available to everyone, or are they too expensive for some families? Are there any other ways for pupils to get extra help?

PREDICTING CONTENT USING VISUALS

2 Look at the pictures from the video. Discuss the questions with a partner.

1 Where do you think these pupils are studying?
2 Who are the pupils in the pictures? Describe them.
3 Which pictures show traditional learning environments? Which ones are less traditional?

GLOSSARY

tutor (n) someone who teachers one person or a very small group of people
catch up on/with (phr v) do something you did not have time for earlier
private tuition (n) a class for a single person, usually for a fee
haves and have-nots (idiom) the rich and the poor
try out (phr v) use something for the first time to see if it works or if you like it
pilot (v) test a new product with a small group or in a small area
level the playing field (idiom) create a situation that is fair for everyone

WHILE WATCHING

UNDERSTANDING MAIN IDEAS

3 Watch the video. Write *T* (true) or *F* (false) next to the statements below. Correct the false statements.

_____ 1 Most students in London get private tuition.
_____ 2 It can be difficult for poor students to find and pay for good tutors.
_____ 3 The app has already helped thousands of students improve their performance in school.

_____ 4 The teachers are not sure that a tuition app is a good idea.

_____ 5 The app provides access to tuition for students who cannot afford private lessons.

_____ 6 If the programme is successful, the app may become available to students all over the UK.

SUMMARIZING

4 Watch again. Use the words and phrases in the box to complete the summary.

access	afford	available	expensive	extra	fall behind

More and more students in the UK are getting [1]__________ help outside class, but private tuition can be quite [2]__________ and not every student can [3]__________ it. Unfortunately, without the extra help, poor students sometimes [4]__________ in their studies. A new app may be able to solve this problem by providing [5]__________ to tuition for all students. If it works in this small programme, it may become [6]__________ to students all over the country.

MAKING INFERENCES

5 Match the ideas to the speakers who might say them.

1 Female student, Sheikh Fahmida Musarrat
2 Chief Executive of the Sutton Trust, Dr Lee Elliot-Major
3 Oakland Schools teacher, Simon Ramsay

a We want schools to use technology to help their pupils.
b This app gives opportunities to all of our students.
c I use the app when my parents can't help me with my schoolwork.
d The app is really useful because our students can use it any time. They don't have to be in school.
e The app is great if you don't have time to ask the teacher for extra help.

DISCUSSION

6 Work with a partner and answer the questions. Give reasons for your answers.

1 What is your view of tuition outside of class? Is it necessary? Should students be able to learn everything in the classroom?
2 Have you ever tried learning something using an app? If so, describe the experience. If not, would you like to try it? Why / Why not?
3 Private tuition may increase the gap between rich and poor. Do you think technology can close it? Why / Why not? How?

READING

READING 1

PREPARING TO READ

UNDERSTANDING KEY VOCABULARY

1 You are going to read an essay about two university subjects. Read the sentences and write the correct form of the words in bold next to the definitions.

1 When you want to support your opinion in an essay, it is good to provide **concrete** examples to support it rather than simply giving your general point of view.
2 In October, the university will **launch** a new programme to use more solar energy.
3 Chemistry and Physics are related, but they are taught as separate scientific **disciplines**.
4 If you want to **pursue** a career in politics, Political science is a good subject to study.
5 Some schools are more **oriented** towards science learning than others.
6 There is a large **gender gap** in Science and Engineering education. However, governments and universities are trying to attract more female students to these subjects.
7 Some people feel that students from lower-income families are **under-represented** at the best universities.
8 As distance education **evolves**, more and more people may get academic degrees online.

a ________ (v) to try to do or achieve
b ________ (adj) based on actual things and particular examples
c ________ (v) to begin something or introduce a new plan
d ________ (adj) directed towards or focused on
e ________ (adj) not given enough presence; in unreasonably lower numbers than others
f ________ (v) to change or develop gradually
g ________ (n) a particular area of study
h ________ (n) the difference in opportunities, attitudes, pay, etc. between men and women

2 Read the sentences. The words and phrases in bold are the *opposites* of the words in bold from Exercise 1. Write the correct form of the words from Exercise 1 next to the opposites below.

1 I started medical school, but it was not right for me, so I decided to **quit** the programme. pursue
2 Cooking is a **non-academic topic** that you cannot study at a major university. ________
3 There is an **equal male-to-female ratio** at my university. ________
4 The university will **end** its marketing campaign in June. ________
5 Mechanical engineering courses are usually **not directed** towards people studying literature. ________
6 Every Physics professor at the university attended the meeting, so that department was a bit **over-represented.** ________
7 You cannot tell what objects the artist is trying to paint in her work. Her paintings are very **abstract**. ________
8 If you do not read the latest research in your field, your career may suffer and **stop developing**. ________

USING YOUR KNOWLEDGE

3 Circle the answers which are true for you. Then compare with a partner. Provide additional information to support your answer.

1 Do you know anyone who has studied or plans to study Business?
a yes b no c not sure
2 Do you know anyone who has studied or plans to study Engineering?
a yes b no c not sure
3 Which one do you think is a more difficult subject to study?
a Engineering b Business c they are equally difficult
4 Which one do you think is better preparation for finding a job after university?
a Engineering b Business c they are equal

UNIVERSITY COURSES: BUSINESS VS ENGINEERING

1 Perhaps the most important decision a university student has to make is what subject to study. Most universities offer a wide variety of interesting subjects from which to choose, so for some students the choice can be difficult. Some university students want to follow their academic interests and study something that is not directly linked to a future career, such as History or Philosophy. Others are looking for a degree in a practical subject that provides **concrete** skills for the working world. For these students, subjects like Business and Engineering are attractive options. Despite this common ground, however, there are significant differences between these two subjects in terms of their popularity and the gender ratio[1] of students.

2 Both Business and Engineering are viewed as subjects which will help students **launch** their careers after graduation, but these **disciplines** also provide a good foundation for continued study in graduate school. Many students who **pursue** an MBA[2] feel that the best way to get into a good programme is to study Business and Management in university. Students who want to get a graduate degree in Engineering will have a hard time with the subject if they have not already taken Engineering courses in university, which is different from degrees more **oriented** towards the humanities[3]. Finally, both areas require the use of mathematics. Business students will need to be able to work with budgets and financial and accounting ideas, and engineers rely on mathematical calculations for their work.

3 On the other hand, these two subjects differ quite a bit – both in terms of their popularity and the presence of a **gender gap**. By all measures, Business is the most popular subject for UK university students overall. Engineering subjects, in contrast, are much less popular. This is despite the fact that engineering-led industry contributes about 40% of the UK's gross domestic product, and is a key component of its national economy. In terms of gender balance, many university courses are commonly more popular with one gender than the other, but Business courses are equally popular with both male and female students. When asked why they have chosen Business, many women say that they want to study something that makes them employable but that also focuses on communication skills. In the case of students studying Engineering and Technology, which have less focus on communication skills, only about 16% of Engineering and Technology students in the UK are female. Engineering and Technology make up two of the four disciplines that form the acronym STEM (Science, Technology, Engineering and Mathematics). There are different theories about why women are so **under-represented** in STEM. Some people think that it is simply because fewer women are interested in the field, while others think that young girls may be discouraged by parents, teachers and society in general from pursuing STEM occupations.

4 To conclude, Business and Engineering are both practical, career-oriented courses that are attractive to British university students, but which differ in significant ways. Business, the most popular subject, has an even split between male and female students. Engineering, in contrast, is less popular with women – 84% of its students are male. As perceptions of men and women continue to change in the UK, and as the job market **evolves**, it will be interesting to see if these trends continue or change.

[1]**gender ratio** (n) the proportion of males to females in a given population or group

[2]**MBA** (Masters of Business Administration) (n) an advanced degree in business

[3]**humanities** (n) literature, language, history, philosophy, and other subjects that are not a science

WHILE READING

READING FOR MAIN IDEAS

4 Read the essay. Then read these facts and tick (✔) if they apply to Business, Engineering or both.

		Business	Engineering	both
1	will help students launch their careers			
2	has a gender gap			
3	is the most popular UK university subject			
4	requires the use of mathematics			
5	provides a good foundation for graduate school			

READING FOR DETAIL

5 Write *T* (true) or *F* (false) next to the statements. Correct the false statements.

_____ 1 Engineering-led industry contributes more than half of the UK's GDP.

____

_____ 2 84% of Engineering students are male.

____

_____ 3 An equal number of men and women want to study Business.

____

_____ 4 There are three STEM subjects.

____

_____ 5 16% of STEM students are female.

____

READING BETWEEN THE LINES

SKILLS

Making inferences

Sometimes writers suggest the meaning of something without saying it directly. Being able to read this inferred meaning (as well as the literal meaning of the words) is a useful skill. Practise using reasoning, logic, and your knowledge of the world to work out the real meaning behind the words you read.

MAKING INFERENCES

6 Work with a partner. Discuss the questions.

1 Why would a student prefer to study a career-oriented subject?
2 What are the disadvantages of studying Business or Engineering?

DISCUSSION

7 Discuss the questions with your partner.

1 Are you interested in STEM subjects? Why / Why not?
2 Are there any subjects in your country which have a significantly higher percentage of male or female students? Why do you think that is?

PLUS

READING 2

PREPARING TO READ

UNDERSTANDING KEY VOCABULARY

1 You are going to read an article about distance learning and face-to-face learning. Before you read, review the collocations and their meanings. Then complete the sentences with your own words.

core principles (n phr) key values
credible alternative (n phr) reliable substitute
distance learning (n phr) general education from online instruction
modern phenomenon (n phr) recent trend
online degree (n phr) an academic qualification obtained from online instruction
significant difference (n phr) important distinction
technological advances (n phr) developments in technology
virtual classroom (n phr) online course

1 One interesting **modern phenomenon** in my country is ______________________ .

2 A subject which might not work well for **distance learning** is ______________________ .

3 One advantage of a real classroom over a **virtual classroom** is ______________________ .

4 One advantage of an **online degree** over a degree which requires attending classes is ______________________ .

5 It's possible that a **credible alternative** to petrol might be ______________________ .

6 Because of **technological advances**, it is now much easier to ______________________ .

7 One of the **core principles** of many universities is ______________________ .

8 One **significant difference** between secondary school and university is ______________________ .

PLUS

USING YOUR KNOWLEDGE

2 Look at the statements below. Do you think they are true (*T*) or false (*F*)?

_____ 1 Distance learning is a new idea.
_____ 2 Distance learning requires good technological access.
_____ 3 Face-to-face learning is better than distance learning.

3 Read the article and check your answers to Exercise 2.

DISTANCE LEARNING VS FACE-TO-FACE LEARNING

1 Although many people think it is a **modern phenomenon**, **distance learning** has been around for at least 200 years in one form or another. Historical examples of long-distance learning include students being sent a series of weekly lessons by mail. The **technological advances** of the past 20 or so years, however, have meant that this form of education is now a **credible alternative** to face-to-face learning. Indeed, 1996 saw the establishment of the world's first 'virtual university' in the United States, showing how far distance learning has come in a relatively short space of time. While it is now possible to obtain a large variety of **online degrees**, which is the best type of education to pursue? A closer examination of this topic reveals that distance and traditional educational instruction have **significant differences** but also some similarities.

2 When comparing the two systems, the most obvious difference lies in the way that instruction is delivered. Distance learning is heavily dependent on technology, particularly the internet. In a face-to-face course, students may only require a computer for the purpose of writing an essay. In comparison, when learning remotely, technology is the principal means of communication. Face-to-face instruction must take place in real time and in one location. Conversely, distance learning can happen at any time and in any location, since the learning is not restricted by geography. The flexibility this provides means that students may be better able to learn at their own pace, but it may also mean that learners have to be well organized and self-disciplined. In other words, they must be more highly motivated in order to do well in distance-learning courses. Finally, with face-to-face learning, the teacher and student have the opportunity to develop a personal relationship. In a **virtual classroom**, by contrast, the teacher may seldom or never actually meet the student. This may make it hard for teachers to understand their students' specific learning needs.

3 Although the nature of the teacher-student relationship may differ in the two methods, they do share the same **core principles**. Just as a teacher is the 'knower' in a classroom, he or she is the one responsible for helping students understand the key sections of an online course. The teacher needs to decide how to best present the material to be learned and in which sequence the topics should be introduced. He or she must also create the assignments for the course and help the students know what resources (textbooks, websites and so on) will best support their learning. Additionally, a teacher needs to provide student feedback in some way. For example, a language teacher in a classroom may be able to correct a student's grammar or pronunciation in the moment, whereas a distance-learning teacher may need to provide written or recorded feedback to be delivered later. In any case, all the usual elements of the teacher's role are necessary, no matter what kind of instruction is being used.

4 It is difficult to state whether one form of learning is better than another, since they are geared towards different learning situations. They are certainly different experiences. Nevertheless, there are strong similarities between the two systems, which can both produce positive results. A student who has the choice should consider the advantages and disadvantages of each method before deciding to take a course.

WHILE READING

READING FOR MAIN IDEAS

4 Write the correct paragraph number (1–4) next to the description.

1 Similarities between the two methods Paragraph: ______
2 General summary and conclusions Paragraph: ______
3 Differences between the methods Paragraph: ______
4 The history and background of the topic Paragraph: ______

READING FOR DETAIL

5 Are the statements about distance learning, face-to-face learning or both? Tick (✔) the correct column.

		distance learning	face-to-face learning	both
1	develops a strong student–teacher relationship			
2	relies heavily on technology			
3	flexible with time			
4	can be an effective way of teaching			
5	requires a high level of motivation			
6	not limited by geography			
7	can suit many types of students			

READING BETWEEN THE LINES

MAKING INFERENCES

6 Work with a partner. Answer the questions based on your understanding of the information in the article.

1 Why is the difference that is mentioned in paragraph 2 called 'obvious'?

______

2 Why can online learning be slightly impersonal?

______

3 Paragraph 3 states that 'all the usual elements of the teacher's role are necessary' in any kind of instruction. What are these elements?

______

4 Do you think this author generally approves or disapproves of distance learning? Why?

______

DISCUSSION

SYNTHESIZING

7 Work with a partner. Use ideas from Reading 1 and Reading 2 to discuss the following questions.

1 Have you ever tried to learn something online? What were the advantages and disadvantages of doing this?
2 Which model of learning do you prefer? Give reasons for your answer.
3 Which do you think would work better with distance learning: a Business course or an Engineering course? Why?

LANGUAGE DEVELOPMENT

EDUCATION VOCABULARY

1 Complete each sentence with a word from the box. Use the Glossary on pages 191–193 to help you.

assignment	degree	dissertation	examination	journal
lecturer	plagiarism	semester	seminar	term	tutor

1 The word for a written essay at university is a(n) ________ .
2 An academic year can be split into three periods, each called a(n) ________ .
3 An academic year can also be divided into two periods, each called a(n) ________ .
4 ________ is when students copy from or do not acknowledge their sources when writing an essay.
5 A(n) ________ is a quarterly, peer-reviewed collection of research papers.
6 A(n) ________ is the holder of a research position at a university who also teaches.
7 A(n) ________ is an occasion when a teacher or expert and a group of people meet to study and discuss something.
8 A(n) ________ assumes responsibility for students' academic and personal welfare.
9 When you have completed a programme of study at a university, you get a(n) ________ .
10 A(n) ________ is a long essay of between 8,000 and 12,000 words.
11 A(n) ________ is a formal test that students must pass to get a specific qualification.

PLUS

ACADEMIC WORDS

2 Match the academic words to the definitions.

1 alternative
2 establishment
3 virtual
4 significant
5 core
6 principle
7 specific
8 motivation
9 aspect

a the act of starting or creating something that will last a long time
b a feature of something
c willingness to do something
d something that is different, especially from what is usual; a choice
e relating to one thing and not others; particular
f similar to real life but existing in a technological environment
g important, large or great
h central, basic
i a basic truth that explains or controls how something happens or works

3 Complete the sentences with the correct form of the words from Exercise 2. You will not use all of the words.

1 Many students prefer to study a job-related subject as a(n) __________ to an academic course.
2 The flexibility offered by distance learning is seen as a(n) __________ benefit by many students.
3 One beneficial __________ of university education is meeting the other students on the course.
4 Tutors work with students to help them understand the key __________ of their courses.
5 Distance learning requires students to have a high level of __________ .
6 Distance learning can make it hard for a teacher to understand a student's __________ learning needs.
7 As well as taking __________ modules, students will be able to take other optional elective classes in various areas.
8 1996 saw the establishment of the world's first __________ university, which operated only on the internet.

PLUS

WRITING

CRITICAL THINKING

At the end of this unit, you are going to write a comparison and contrast essay. Look at this unit's writing task below.

> Discuss the various similarities and differences between studying a language and studying Mathematics.

UNDERSTAND

1 Look at the two ideas maps below. One is labelled 'studying a language' and the other 'studying Mathematics'. Add details according to your experience of studying these subjects.

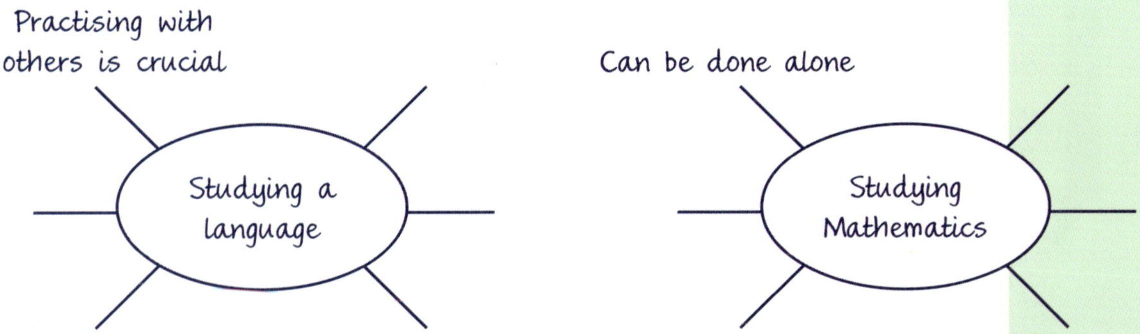

SKILLS

Analyzing similarities and differences

In academic discourse, it is often important to compare and contrast information to see the similarities and differences between topics or ideas. A Venn diagram is a very common way of doing this. Use the Venn diagram to discuss the various similarities and differences between studying a language and studying Maths.

ANALYZE

2 Write the information from the ideas maps in Exercise 1 into the appropriate parts of the Venn diagram. Try to get at least three pieces of information in each of the three sections. Do more research online to add new information.

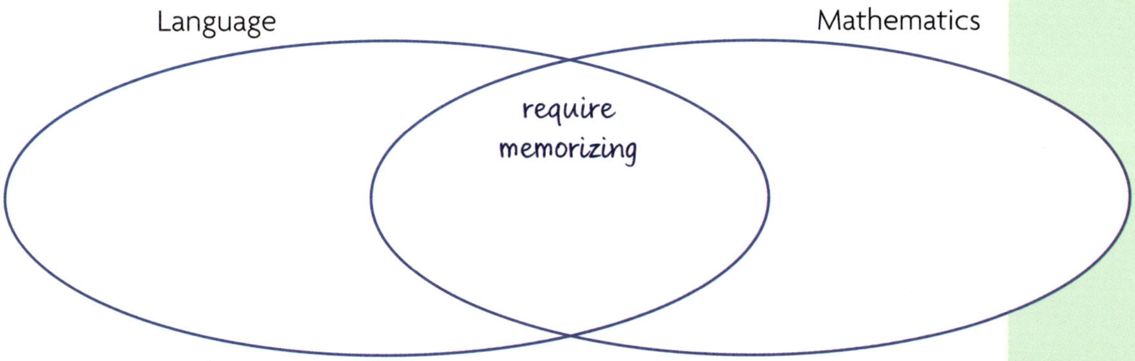

3 Compare your Venn diagram with a partner. Are there any good ideas which you could add to yours?

GRAMMAR FOR WRITING

COMPARISON AND CONTRAST LANGUAGE

GRAMMAR

Transitions to show comparison and contrast

The ability to compare similar ideas or to contrast different ideas is an important skill in academic writing. This is especially true when writers are asked to discuss a subject before giving an opinion. Use a comma after transition words and phrases when they begin a sentence.

Comparison		Contrast	
Similarly, …	*In the same way, …*	*However, …*	*In contrast, …*
Likewise, …		*Conversely, …*	*On the other hand, …*

Students in face-to-face courses see tutors often. **Similarly**, students in distance-learning courses contact their tutors in online forums often.

Universities charge high tuition fees for academic subjects. **However**, colleges charge much less for vocational courses.

1 Complete the sentences with a transition word or phrase from the box. More than one answer may be possible.

conversely	in contrast	in the same way	similarly

1 If your native language is Swedish, then learning Danish is not very difficult. ______________ , Mandarin will be challenging to learn.
2 Algebra is a Maths subject which many students learn in secondary school. ______________ , Geometry is commonly taught at secondary school level.
3 The most common second language for British students to learn is French. ______________ , the most common second language for French students to study is English.
4 Language learning requires memorizing and practising vocabulary. ______________ , Maths involves memorizing and practising formulas.

2 Complete the sentences with your own ideas to compare or contrast.

1 Academic subjects such as Law lead to high-paying careers. In contrast, ______________________________
2 Medicine involves both academic and professionally related aspects. Similarly, ______________________________
3 Theoretical courses tend not to prepare students for the real world. Conversely, ______________________________
4 Vocational training can be learned by taking special courses. Likewise, ______________________________

GRAMMAR

Adverb clauses of contrast

Adverb clauses of contrast are used mainly to contrast two things or ideas. You can show contrast in the topic sentence of a paragraph or in the thesis statement of an essay by using an adverb clause. An adverb clause has a subject and a verb, but it is not a complete sentence. It begins with the words *while* or *whereas*. In sentences expressing contrast, *while* and *whereas* have the same meaning.

While/Whereas teachers and parents both have a child's interests at heart, they are different because they may not have the same expectations of the child.

The main difference between teachers and parents is that teachers are paid, **while/whereas parents are not**.

An adverb clause of contrast can come before or after the main clause. If it comes first, it is followed by a comma. In academic writing, it is more common for adverb clauses of contrast to appear second. Unlike other adverb clauses, a comma can come before an adverb clause of contrast when it appears second to emphasize contrast.

A language teacher in a classroom may be able to correct a student's grammar or pronunciation in the moment, **while/whereas a distance-learning teacher may need to provide written or recorded feedback to be delivered later**.

While/Whereas a distance-learning teacher may need to provide written or recorded feedback to be delivered later, a language teacher in a classroom may be able to correct a student's grammar or pronunciation in the moment.

3 Combine the sentences using adverb clauses of contrast with *while* or *whereas*. For some items, more than one answer is possible.

1 Academic courses focus on subjects like Maths, Science and Literature. Vocational courses focus on practical skills.

____

____

2 A university is a very large institution which offers undergraduate and graduate degrees. A college is a smaller institution which typically offers only undergraduate degrees.

____

____

3 Academic courses are theoretical. Vocational subjects are not.

____

____

4 More men tend to graduate with degrees in Maths or Science. More women tend to graduate with degrees in languages or Literature.

____

____

4 Circle the sentence which uses the adverb clause correctly. Pay attention to sentence structure and punctuation.

1 **a** Biology is a science subject whereas, History is a humanities subject.
  b Biology is a science subject, whereas History is a humanities subject.

2 **a** While taking a pre-university foundation year in the UK is common for international students. It is not common in the US.
  b While taking a pre-university foundation year in the UK is common for international students, it is not common in the US.

3 **a** While certain teachers prefer to provide written comments on students' writing, others prefer to hold face-to-face conferences.
  b Certain teachers prefer to provide written comments on students' writing. While others prefer to hold face-to-face conferences.

5 Add appropriate punctuation to these sentences.

1 Some professions only require a Bachelor's Degree while others require a graduate degree.

2 Whereas Japanese students can get a bachelor's degree in Law Canadian students cannot.

3 While Business is considered a university subject that will lead to job offers Philosophy is usually not.

6 Complete the sentences with an appropriate ending.

1 While some students choose to go to university, ______________________________
____
____
____.

2 Engineering study requires good mathematics skills, whereas ______________
____
____
____.

3 Some universities require students to study both STEM and humanities subjects, whereas ______________________________________
____
____
____.

ACADEMIC WRITING SKILLS

AVOIDING RUN-ON SENTENCES AND COMMA SPLICES

Run-on sentences and comma splices are common errors that writers must know how to avoid in academic writing.

Run-on sentences

Run-on sentences are incorrect because they have two independent clauses which have not been connected in the right way.

independent clause | *independent clause*

✘ Engineering and Business are both popular subjects they both use mathematics.

To fix a run-on sentence, you can:

- add a comma and a coordinating conjunction like *and*, *but* or *so*.
  Engineering and Business are both popular subjects, **and** they both use mathematics.
- separate the clauses with a semicolon.
  Engineering and Business are both popular subjects; they both use mathematics.
- make the clauses into two separate sentences.
  Engineering and Business are both popular subjects. They both use mathematics.

Comma splices

Comma splices are two independent clauses connected only with a comma.

✘ Business is a more popular subject than Engineering, it also has a smaller gender gap.

As with run-on sentences, you can correct comma splices by adding a coordinating conjunction (such as *and*, *but* or *so*), separating the clauses with a semicolon, or making the clauses two separate sentences.

Business is a more popular subject than Engineering, **and** it also has a smaller gender gap.
Business is a more popular subject than Engineering; it also has a smaller gender gap.
Business is a more popular subject than Engineering. It also has a smaller gender gap.

SKILLS

1 Identify the run-on sentences or comma splices in the sentences. Write *C* (comma splice) or *R* (run-on sentence). Then correct the sentences.

1 Many students study a second language some students study a third language. ______
2 Engineering is a popular university course, it is not as popular as Business. ______
3 Maths focuses on numbers language learning focuses on words. ______
4 Distance learning has become very popular you can even earn a degree this way. ______
5 Some students prefer to study academic subjects other students prefer vocational courses. ______
6 All universities charge tuition fees some are more expensive than others. ______

PLUS

2 Correct the sentences below – some are run-ons, some have comma splices.

1 Not everyone needs to go to university there are some rewarding careers that do not require university degrees.
2 The two oldest universities in the UK are Oxford and Cambridge, they were both founded in the Middle Ages.
3 Students getting PhD degrees work as research assistants it is part of their arrangement with the university.
4 The experience of going to university is not just an academic one, students also make valuable lifelong friendships there.

COMPARISON AND CONTRAST ESSAYS

SKILLS

One common way to structure a comparison and contrast essay is to start with a discussion about the differences between the two subjects and then follow with a discussion about the similarities.

Introductory paragraph:
- gives some background on the two subjects of comparison
- provides a thesis statement which explains whether the writer feels that the differences or similarities are more important, or just that they both exist

Body paragraph 1: states the differences between subject 1 and subject 2

Body paragraph 2: states the similarities between subject 1 and subject 2

Concluding paragraph:
- restates the thesis
- ends with a comment showing the writer's opinion

3 Look back at Readings 1 and 2. Answer the questions with a partner.

1 In Reading 1, does the thesis statement indicate that the author will emphasize the *differences* of the subjects, the *similarities* of the subjects or that both differences and similarities exist?
2 In Reading 2, does the thesis statement indicate that the author will emphasize the *differences* of the subjects, the *similarities* of the subjects or that both differences and similarities exist?
3 In the explanation of comparison and contrast essays which was just presented, the suggested structure of the body paragraphs is that the first discusses differences and the second discusses similarities. Which reading (1 or 2) follows this structure?

WRITING TASK

Discuss the various similarities and differences between studying a language and studying Mathematics.

PLAN

1 Look back at the Venn diagram in Critical thinking with your notes on the similarities and differences between studying a language and studying Mathematics. Now take those ideas, plus any new ones you can think of, and create an outline for your essay using the structure below. Try to include at least three points for each body paragraph.

Introductory paragraph:	background information, thesis statement
Body paragraph 1:	differences
Body paragraph 2:	similarities
Concluding paragraph:	your opinion

2 Write a thesis statement for your essay. You can use an adverb clause with *while* or *whereas* to show contrast.

3 Refer to the Task checklist on page 56 as you plan your essay.

WRITE A FIRST DRAFT

4 Write your essay using the outline. Write 350–400 words.

REVISE

5 Use the Task checklist to review your essay for content and structure.

TASK CHECKLIST	✔
Did you give background information and a thesis statement in your introduction?	
Do you have one body paragraph about the differences and another body paragraph about the similarities?	
Did you use examples to strengthen your arguments in the body paragraphs?	
Did you restate the thesis statement and give your opinion in the conclusion?	

6 Make any necessary changes to your essay.

EDIT

7 Use the Language checklist to edit your essay for language errors.

LANGUAGE CHECKLIST	✔
Did you use comparison and contrast language correctly?	
Did you use adverb clauses to show contrast correctly?	
Did you use a range of academic words?	
Did you use collocations correctly?	
Did you avoid run-on sentences and comma splices?	

8 Make any necessary changes to your essay.

OBJECTIVES REVIEW

1 Check your learning objectives for this unit. Write *3*, *2* or *1* for each objective.

3 = very well 2 = well 1 = not so well

I can ...

watch and understand a video about an app that helps children catch up outside the classroom.	_____
make inferences.	_____
analyze similarities and differences.	_____
use a Venn diagram to plan a comparison-contrast essay.	_____
use transitions to show comparison and contrast.	_____
use adverb clauses of contrast.	_____
avoid run-on sentences and comma splices.	_____
write a comparison and contrast essay.	_____

2 Use the *Unlock* Digital Workbook for more practice with this unit's learning objectives.

UNLOCK ONLINE

WORDLIST

alternative (n) ⊙
aspect (n) ⊙
assignment (n) ⊙
concrete (adj) ⊙
core (adj) ⊙
core principles (n phr)
credible alternative (n phr)
degree (n) ⊙
discipline (n) ⊙
dissertation (n) ⊙
distance learning (n phr)
establishment (n) ⊙
evolve (v) ⊙
examination (n) ⊙
gender gap (n phr)
journal (n) ⊙
launch (v)
lecturer (n)
modern phenomenon (n phr)
motivation (n) ⊙
online degree (n phr)
oriented (adj) ⊙
plagiarism (n)
principle (adj) ⊙
pursue (v) ⊙
semester (n)
seminar (n)
significant (adj) ⊙
significant difference (n phr)
specific (adj) ⊙
technological advances (n phr)
term (n) ⊙
tutor (n)
under-represented (adj)
virtual (adj) ⊙
virtual classroom (n phr)

⊙ = high-frequency words in the Cambridge Academic Corpus

LEARNING OBJECTIVES	IN THIS UNIT YOU WILL ...
Watch and listen	watch and understand a video about robots used in surgery.
Reading skill	annotate a text.
Critical thinking	evaluate ideas.
Grammar	use articles; use transitions to show concession.
Academic writing skill	use sentence variety.
Writing task	write an opinion essay.

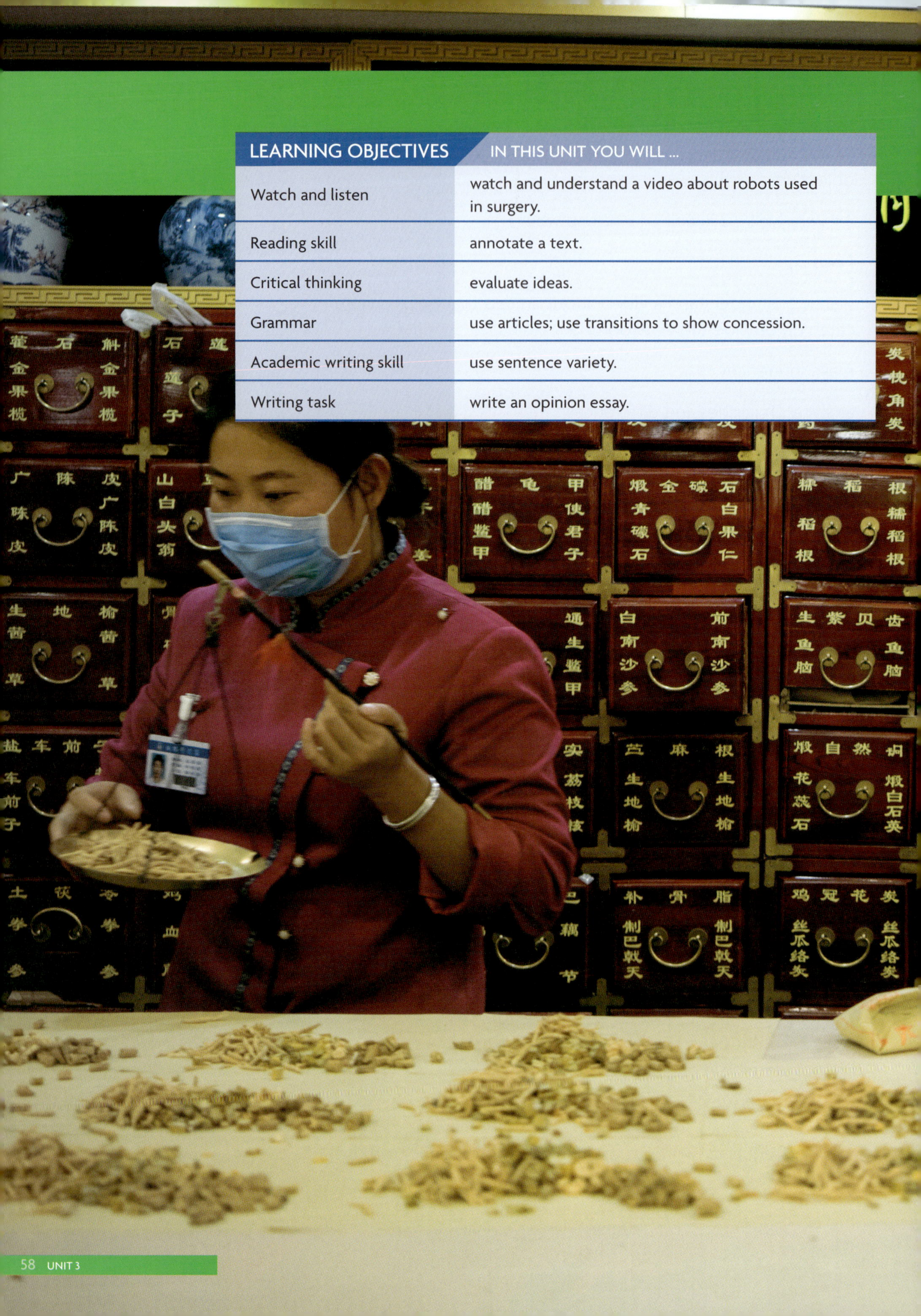

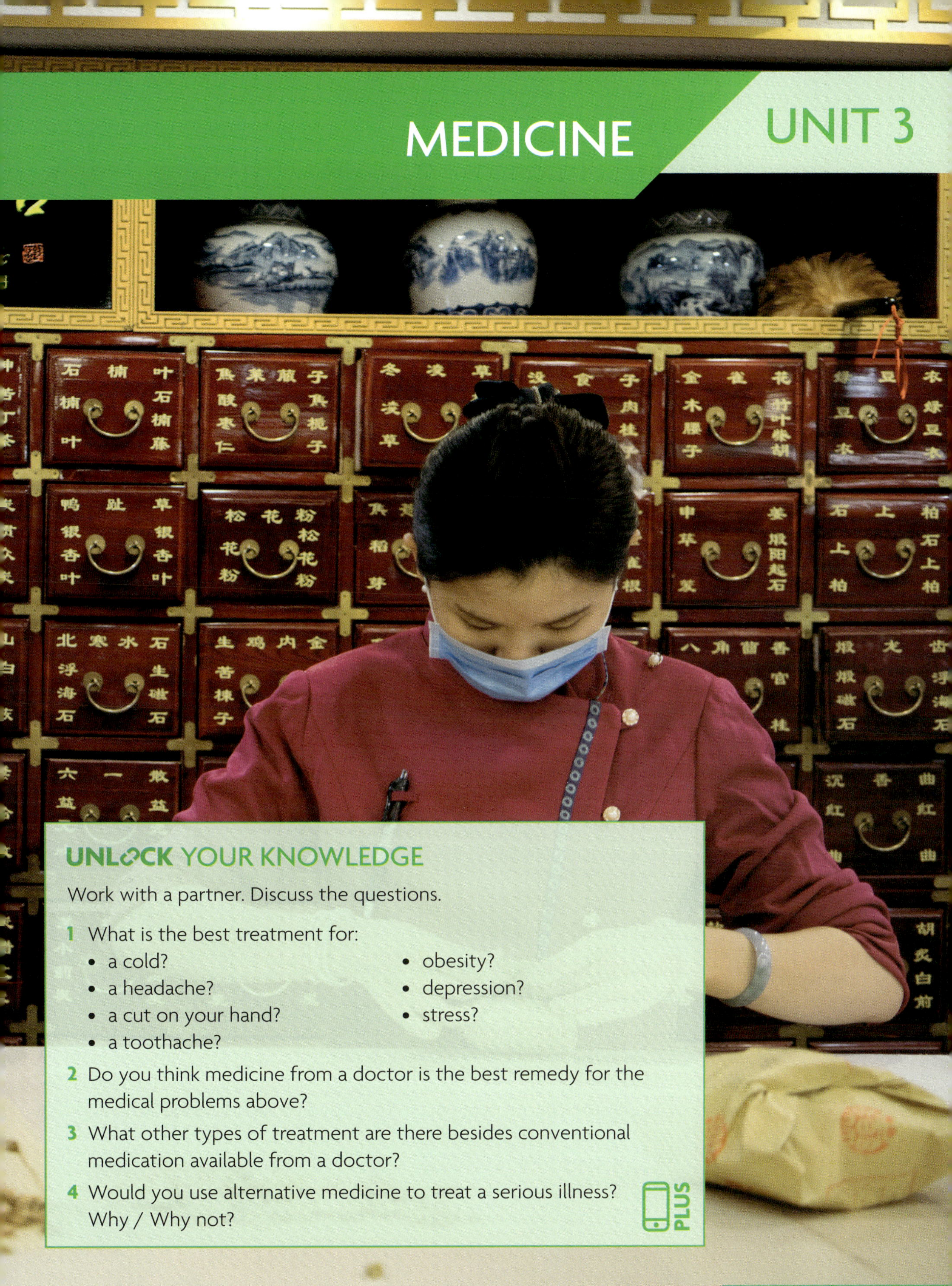

UNIT 3

MEDICINE

UNLOCK YOUR KNOWLEDGE

Work with a partner. Discuss the questions.

1 What is the best treatment for:
- a cold?
- a headache?
- a cut on your hand?
- a toothache?
- obesity?
- depression?
- stress?

2 Do you think medicine from a doctor is the best remedy for the medical problems above?

3 What other types of treatment are there besides conventional medication available from a doctor?

4 Would you use alternative medicine to treat a serious illness? Why / Why not?

PLUS

WATCH AND LISTEN

PREPARING TO WATCH

ACTIVATING YOUR KNOWLEDGE

1 Work with a partner and answer the questions.

1 In what fields are robots used today?
2 What can robots do better than humans?
3 In what ways do you think a robot could help doctors and surgeons?

PREDICTING CONTENT USING VISUALS

2 Look at the pictures from the video. Discuss the questions with a partner.

1 What do all the pictures have in common?
2 What is happening in the first two pictures?
3 What do you notice about the man in the third picture?
4 What do you think the machine in the last picture is making?

GLOSSARY

with the naked eye (n phr) without the help of special equipment (microscope, telescope, etc.)

incision (n) a sharp cut in the body during surgery

bionic digits (n) fingers made of electronics and other man-made materials

NHS (abbr) National Health Service – the UK's public health service

worlds apart (phr) completely different

WHILE WATCHING

UNDERSTANDING MAIN IDEAS

3 Watch the video. Write *T* (true) or *F* (false) or *DNS* (does not say) next to the statements below.

_____ 1 Robotic surgeons have many advantages over human surgeons.
_____ 2 The robotic arm allows the surgeon to identify damaged brain tissue.
_____ 3 The robotic arm which the surgeons use inside the patient's brain is very sensitive.
_____ 4 With new technology, surgeons can operate on single cells.
_____ 5 3D printers can produce bionic arms and fingers.
_____ 6 3D printers have brought down the cost of bionic body parts.

4 Watch again. For each main idea, add supporting details.

UNDERSTANDING DETAIL

1 Robotic surgeons help human surgeons in many ways.

____

2 Shrinking technology has produced tiny robots that can work at the micro-level.

____

3 Robots have changed the life of people who have lost hands or arms.

____

4 With 3D printing, the cost of bionics is within the reach of ordinary people.

____

5 Work with a partner. Discuss the questions. Give reasons for your answers.

MAKING INFERENCES

1 The video mentions several things that the robotic surgeon does well. What might be some others?
2 Dr Yang says that with micro-robotics, there is no need to make an incision. Why is this a positive feature?
3 The current cost of bionics is beyond the reach of NHS patients. Who is probably receiving bionic limbs now?
4 Why do you think that 3D printing is cheaper than other manufacturing processes?

DISCUSSION

6 Work with a partner and answer the questions.

1 Who do you trust more: robotic or human surgeons? Give reasons for your answer.
2 Do you think there will be a time when humans are not involved in surgery at all? Why / Why not?
3 What impact do you think 3D printing will have in other fields, for example, manufacturing?

READING

READING 1

PREPARING TO READ

UNDERSTANDING KEY VOCABULARY

1 Read the sentences and choose the best definition for the words in bold.

1 After my knee **surgery**, my leg was sore for several weeks.
   a taking medicine for a period of time after you are sick
   b the cutting open of the body to repair a damaged part
2 Two **symptoms** of the common cold are coughing and sneezing.
   a types of illnesses
   b reactions or feelings of illness which are caused by a disease
3 Doctors are usually big **proponents** of regular exercise for their patients as exercise can have many positive effects on health.
   a people who support a particular idea or plan of action
   b people who argue against an idea
4 The new treatment is **controversial**. Some people think it has not been tested enough, while others believe in it.
   a causing disagreement or discussion
   b causing agreement
5 The government has **funded** the hospital in my neighbourhood by donating £5 million of last year's tax money.
   a given land for a new building
   b provided money to pay for something
6 It is dangerous to consume illegal **substances** because they have not been approved by the country's medical authorities.
   a foods which are unhealthy
   b materials with particular physical characteristics
7 My grandmother is afraid to use **conventional** treatment for her illness. Instead, she drinks a tea made from a variety of plants.
   a following the usual practices
   b alternative and non-traditional
8 Heart disease is the **chief** cause of death for people in the United States. It kills more people than any other disease.
   a most important or main
   b most uncommon

2 You are going to read an article about the homeopathy debate. Look quickly at the article. Look at the title, subheads and introduction. Decide which statement best describes what the article is about.

1 The article presents the arguments for and against conventional types of medicine.
2 The article discusses why some alternative medical treatments are free.
3 The article gives two people's opinions on the effectiveness of using homeopathy.
4 The article discusses a range of alternative medical treatments.

SKIMMING

WHILE READING

SKILLS

Annotating a text

Annotating a text while you read can help you remember information a lot better. When you annotate, you mark up the text and add notes in the margin as you read. When you read about different writers' opinions on a single subject, it is a good idea to highlight each writer's opinions in a different colour, then underline the support each writer gives for their opinions. You can also react to a writer's opinions by writing notes in the margin, putting a star next to the strongest reasons and support, etc.

3 Read the article on the homeopathy debate. Highlight each writer's opinion in a different colour and underline the support each writer provides. Write notes in the margin as you read.

ANNOTATING

4 Read the article again. Write *T* (true), *F* (false) or *DNS* (does not say) next to the statements. Correct the false statements.

READING FOR DETAIL

_____ 1 The majority of countries use alternative rather than conventional medicine.
_____ 2 Supporters of homeopathy believe that patients should have choices in their treatment.
_____ 3 More than two-thirds of doctors in the UK are against state-funded homeopathic treatment.
_____ 4 Traditional Indian doctors frequently use homeopathy.
_____ 5 Abigail Hayes thinks that homeopathic remedies only work because of the placebo effect.
_____ 6 In the UK, people currently have a choice as to what treatment they can get.
_____ 7 Homeopathic healthcare is not available in the United States.
_____ 8 Weak, highly diluted liquids are a common form of homeopathic treatment.

The homeopathy debate

1 Most national health systems use **conventional** medicine, meaning that illnesses are treated using drugs and **surgery**. However, there is also a range of alternative medical treatments to choose from. One **controversial** treatment is homeopathy. Homeopathic remedies are highly diluted[1] mixtures of natural **substances,** such as plants and minerals, which may cause the **symptoms** of a disease in healthy people. The idea is that they will cure similar symptoms in sick people. Supporters of homeopathy believe that it can be effective. Others argue, however, that homeopathy does not work and agree that the state should not **fund** it. Here, one **proponent** and one critic present their cases.

Homeopathy should be state funded
by Abigail Hayes (Professional Homeopath)

2 The British National Health Service was founded to provide free healthcare to people who needed it. Since it was founded in 1948, patients have been able to get homeopathic treatment, and there's no good reason why this shouldn't continue. Most importantly, it's estimated that homeopathic treatments only cost the NHS between £4–10 million a year. This is a fraction of the cost paid out to conventional drug companies. Also, but perhaps less importantly, over 400 doctors regularly recommend homeopathic treatments. Since they are cheap and popular, I find it difficult to understand why the government is considering cutting funding for them. Why shouldn't people be allowed to make their own health choices? They have this freedom in other aspects of their lives – for example, which school to send their children to – so why not in terms of their healthcare?

Homeopathic treatments: not too expensive, allow patient choice, effective, use 'power of belief'

3 As for the critics who argue that homeopathy doesn't work, I could give hundreds of examples of patients who have been cured by my treatment. On top of that, there's plenty of research which shows the benefits it can bring. Homeopathy wouldn't have survived so long if it were complete nonsense. It has much more than just a placebo effect[2]. Too much emphasis is sometimes put on providing 'proof' of why something works. Belief is just as powerful.

Homeopathy should not be state funded
by Dr Piers Wehner (NHS General Practitioner)

4 We don't really know whether homeopathy helps people feel better because of the remedies themselves or because people believe they will work. Some people just feel better when they get personal care and attention from their homeopathic practitioner. For me and many others in my profession, there is absolutely no proof that says homeopathic treatment works. The government's **chief** scientist confirmed this when he said there was 'no real evidence' to support homeopathy. We live in difficult economic times, and every penny the government spends should be checked to ensure that it is not wasted. In fact, 75% of British doctors are against the state funding of homeopathy.

5 One of the main arguments put forward by supporters of homeopathy is that this therapy doesn't cause any damage. However, people may think they are treating their illness by taking homeopathic remedies when there is actually no scientific evidence that this is true. Even more seriously, patients who rely on homeopathy alone for treating life-threatening illnesses like cancer could be taking a big risk. The cancer might no longer be treatable by proven methods if the patient has waited too long trying homeopathy. This can cost lives.

[1]**diluted** (adj) made weaker by mixing with something else, such as water
[2]**placebo effect** (n) an improvement in a patient's condition caused only by his or her belief in the benefit of the treatment

IDENTIFYING OPINIONS

5 Which of the two people in the article would agree with the statements?

		Abigail Hayes	Piers Wehner
1	The doctor says it's too late to help her now. If only she'd gone to see him earlier.		
2	Look, if I don't want to risk the side effects of conventional drugs, why should I have to?		
3	When I see proper clinical trials which prove the effectiveness of homeopathy, *then* I'll change my mind.		
4	The mind has incredibly strong healing powers.		
5	If it means we could stop paying all that money for drugs, then I'm for it.		
6	It worked. I don't know why. It doesn't seem possible, but I'm just happy that it worked.		
7	This is serious. You can keep taking the homeopathic treatment as well, if you want, but you've got to see a doctor.		
8	If three-quarters of professionals are against it, I'm against it.		

READING BETWEEN THE LINES

MAKING INFERENCES

6 Work with a partner. Discuss possible reasons for the statements. Then say whether you agree with them or not.

1 Homeopathic treatment is much cheaper than conventional medicine.
2 Belief is as powerful as medicine.
3 Personal care and attention make people feel better.
4 There is no real proof that homeopathy works.
5 Doctors need to see scientific evidence.

DISCUSSION

7 Work with a partner. Discuss the questions.

1 Why do you think alternative medicines are popular with some people?
2 Do you think alternative medicine only creates a placebo effect?
3 Have you ever used alternative medicine? If not, would you consider doing so? Why / Why not?

PLUS

READING 2

PREPARING TO READ

UNDERSTANDING KEY VOCABULARY

1 You are going to read an article about different types of healthcare systems. Read the definitions. Complete the sentences with the correct form of the words in bold.

burden (n) a duty or responsibility which is hard to bear
consultation (n) a meeting to discuss something or to get advice
contribution (n) an amount of money that is given to help pay for something
labour (n) workers, especially people who do practical work with their hands
regardless (adv) despite; not being affected by something
safety net (n phr) something used to protect a person against possible hardship or difficulty
treatment (n) the use of drugs, exercise, etc. to improve the condition of a sick or injured person, or to cure a disease

1 When elderly people get sick, it sometimes places a financial ________ on their adult children, who have to help pay for expensive treatments.
2 After three months of ________ , the patient can now walk well.
3 Everybody must pay their share, ________ of how much they earn.
4 It is a good idea to save some money as a ________ , just in case you lose your job.
5 The doctor examined me when I went to her for a ________ about my symptoms.
6 We each gave a ________ to send our sick colleague some flowers.
7 When you calculate the price of building a new hospital, you have to consider materials and also the cost of ________ .

PLUS

USING YOUR KNOWLEDGE

2 Work with a partner. Answer the questions.

1 Do you have to pay for healthcare in your country?
2 What healthcare provision, if any, does your government pay for?
3 Should everybody be able to access free healthcare?

SKIMMING

3 Skim the article. Read the title, introduction and topic sentences. Decide which statement best describes what the article is about.

1 The article examines different kinds of public healthcare in different countries.
2 The article focuses on private funding as it relates to healthcare.
3 The article criticizes government policies.
4 The article discusses the role of medication in healthcare.

SHOULD HEALTHCARE BE FREE?

1 Who pays for healthcare? The answer varies from country to country. While in some nations it is completely free for all residents, in others people often receive their health insurance through their employer. There are also places where you can only see a doctor if you pay. Often, a patient is faced with the choice of medium-quality but cheap care versus high-quality but expensive care. Unfortunately, providing healthcare to an entire nation of citizens is a complicated matter. While different healthcare systems have various advantages and disadvantages, no system is ideal.

Free or public healthcare

2 Within the countries which provide free public healthcare, there are many models. In some countries, **consultations**, **treatment** and medicines are free to all citizens. This may be paid for directly by the government, perhaps funded by the country's valuable natural resources that the government owns. Other countries collect money from citizens through taxes based on their income. Workers pay according to how much they earn, and employers also make a **contribution**. Hospitals and other medical services are then provided and run by the government. There may also be some private medical services which people can choose to buy. The advantage of systems such as these is clear: free basic healthcare for all, **regardless** of income. However, it is a very expensive system and, as life expectancy and costs rise, many countries are facing either an unsustainable financial **burden**, or a drop in the quality of services and facilities provided.

Private healthcare

3 In countries where citizens use private providers, healthcare is only available to patients who pay for it, and healthcare providers are commercial companies. In wealthier countries, most citizens take out health insurance to cover their potential medical costs. However, not everyone can afford this, and some governments have a scheme which gives financial assistance to those who need urgent medical care but are unable to afford it. In other nations, there is no such **safety net**, and those who cannot pay simply do not get the healthcare they need, unless they can get help. The disadvantages of this system are obvious: not only are individuals deprived of the medical attention they need, but also the lack of preventative medicine means that infectious diseases can quickly spread. One advantage, however, is that commercial organizations can sometimes provide higher-quality care than struggling government-funded ones.

A mixed system

4 In many countries, there is a mix of public and private funding. This system requires all its citizens to take out health insurance. This is deducted from salaries by the employer, who also has to make a contribution for each worker. Citizens are able to choose their healthcare providers, which may be public or private. However, in some systems, private companies are not permitted to make a profit from providing basic healthcare. This model provides more flexibility than either the public or private models, and ensures access to healthcare for all. However, it has been criticized for driving up the cost of **labour**, which can lead to unemployment.

Conclusion

5 Most of us will likely agree that no healthcare system is perfect. Several countries are now considering a combination of the models for their national health systems. The challenge is to find a system which provides a high-quality level of healthcare to all citizens, but which is also affordable and practical. Whether or not such a system can work remains to be seen.

WHILE READING

READING FOR MAIN IDEAS

4 Answer the questions.

1 Which of the three systems described is most similar to the one your country follows? Are there any differences?
2 Which system gives people the best access to healthcare? The best quality healthcare?

READING FOR DETAIL

5 Read the article again. Identify which system (public, private or mixed) in the article these countries use.

1 **The United Kingdom** Under this country's National Health Service (NHS), all workers pay National Insurance according to how much they earn. This is collected by the government and is used to pay for hospitals and other medical treatment. Most of this is free, except for prescriptions in England, eye care and dental care. Most hospitals are owned and run by the government.
2 **The Democratic Republic of Congo** Here, many people do not have access to a doctor and in some areas there is an insufficient supply of medicine. Doctors are typically paid in cash, and even those who do manage to see a doctor often cannot afford the treatment.
3 **The United Arab Emirates** This country spends more on healthcare per person than almost all of its neighbouring countries in the Gulf region. Healthcare is free (or almost free) for everyone. This is paid for by the government.
4 **The United States** Here, healthcare is expensive. More than 10% of Americans do not have health coverage. Those who are not enrolled in government schemes usually have to pay for some kind of health insurance.
5 **Germany** Here, most workers have to pay for government health insurance from their salaries or buy insurance on their own.

SCANNING TO FIND KEY WORDS

6 Scan the article quickly to find words to complete the table.

synonyms of *people*	
synonyms of *money*	
related to *healthcare*	

READING BETWEEN THE LINES

MAKING INFERENCES

7 Work with a partner. Answer the questions based on information in the article.

1 Which healthcare system might a person with a long-term illness prefer? Why?
2 Which system might a person with a high income prefer? Why?

DISCUSSION

SYNTHESIZING

8 Work with a partner. Use ideas from Reading 1 and Reading 2 to discuss the following questions.

1 Why do you think different countries have different healthcare systems?
2 Do you know of any healthcare treatments that people sometimes use in your country which might be considered alternative or unconventional?
3 In countries where the government pays for everyone's healthcare, do you think alternative treatments such as homeopathy should be covered? Why / Why not?

LANGUAGE DEVELOPMENT

MEDICAL VOCABULARY

1 Read the definitions. Complete the sentences with the correct form of the words in bold.

> **drug dependency** (n phr) being unable to function normally without a particular type of medicine
> **epidemic** (n) an illness which affects large numbers of people at the same time
> **patent** (n) the official legal right to make or sell an invention for a particular number of years
> **preventable illness** (n phr) a disease which can be avoided, often by a person looking after themselves better
> **sedentary lifestyle** (n phr) a way of life which does not involve much activity or exercise
> **underfunding** (n) the lack of money provided for something, often academic or scientific research

1 Following a national emergency such as an earthquake, clean water must be restored quickly to prevent the spread of a(n) ____________ .
2 A decrease in spending by the government means hospitals suffer from ____________ .
3 ____________ can occur when people are prescribed a medicine for a long time.
4 The rise in obesity, particularly among young people, is often the result of a(n) ____________ .
5 A lack of exercise and eating the wrong food can lead to the development of a(n) ____________ such as diabetes.
6 Pharmaceutical companies have ____________ on their new drugs, but once these have expired, other companies can manufacture and market the same drugs.

PLUS

ACADEMIC VOCABULARY

2 Write the correct adjective forms of the academic nouns in the table.

adjective	definition	noun
1	having a negative or harmful effect on something	adversity
2	having the qualities that you connect with trained and skilled people	profession
3	against the law	illegality
4	connected with the body	physicality
5	difficult to understand or find an answer to because of having many different parts	complexity
6	enough or satisfactory for a particular purpose	adequacy
7	traditional and ordinary	convention
8	exact and accurate	precision
9	related to the treatment of illness and injuries	medicine

3 Circle the correct word to complete each sentence.

1 Many countries are fighting against the growing use of *complex* / *illegal* drugs.
2 Doctors and nurses are two examples of *precise* / *professional* healthcare practitioners.
3 People have the right to expect *illegal* / *adequate* service from doctors and nurses.
4 *Conventional* / *Professional* medicine involves the use of drugs, unlike alternative forms of medicine.
5 Several surgeons may be needed in *complex* / *adverse* medical operations.
6 Health systems should focus on the treatment of mental conditions, as well as *physical* / *conventional* healthcare.
7 Hospitals can suffer *illegal* / *adverse* conditions such as underfunding or overcrowding.
8 It takes many years of *medical* / *professional* study to become a doctor.
9 When giving drugs to patients, it is crucially important that the quantity provided is *adequate* / *precise*.

PLUS

WRITING

CRITICAL THINKING

At the end of this unit, you will write an opinion essay. Look at this unit's writing task below.

Is disease prevention the responsibility of individuals and their families, or of the government?

REMEMBER

1 Brainstorm different ways in which diseases can be prevented. Write a separate point next to each number.

1	6
2	7
3	8
4	9
5	10

2 Compare your answers with a partner. Add any useful points to your own list.

EVALUATE

3 Look at the Likert scale below. Think about whose responsibility it is to prevent diseases that affect people in your society: the government, individuals, or somewhere in between. Circle the number which corresponds to your view.

4 Compare your answers with a partner. Do you agree or disagree? Discuss and make any changes you feel are necessary.

1	2	3	4	5	6	7
100% responsibility of the individual			shared responsibility of both			100% responsibility of the government

ANALYZE

5 Look at the work you did in Exercises 1 and 3 on page 71 and answer these questions.

1 Do you think that the government or individuals should be more responsible for preventing diseases?
2 Will the items you have listed be practical or easy to achieve for the individuals? for the government?

6 Work in groups. Look at the list of actions that people can take to avoid becoming sick. Try to agree on the five most important actions.

> avoiding sunburn brushing your teeth
> doing what makes you happy drinking enough water
> eating healthy food getting enough fresh air
> getting recommended vaccinations getting regular exercise
> not smoking reducing stress sleeping enough
> washing your hands frequently

7 Look at your list of the five most important actions and answer the questions.

1 How can individuals and families help themselves to take these actions?
2 How can the government help people to take these actions?

8 Read the statements. Which statements are in favour of individual responsibility for preventative healthcare? Which are against?

1 Healthcare is extremely expensive for governments, and medical evidence strongly suggests that lifestyle is a major indicator of health.
2 People should be able to choose their own lifestyle.
3 People have different situations, so they need to decide what is most beneficial for them.
4 Many people want to eat healthily, but they get tempted by advertising for junk food.
5 Some people cannot afford to use gyms and other sports facilities.
6 Health advice changes so frequently that people need help to know what they should and should not do.
7 The easiest thing is to do nothing, which means many people do not take the steps needed to improve their health.
8 Health education is needed, and not only in schools.
9 If people do not take personal responsibility, they will lose the ability to make good choices.

GRAMMAR FOR WRITING

ARTICLES

GRAMMAR

Articles are some of the most common words in the English language. Knowing how to use them properly is therefore important to the accuracy of academic writing. The way that English uses articles is different from some other languages, but there are some rules you can follow.

Definite article (*the*)

a *The* is used to refer to something specific which has been mentioned before:
Malaria is a disease which affects certain countries. **The disease** is spread by mosquitoes.

b *The* is used for nouns when there is only one example of something:
The US healthcare policy changed in 2014.
The NHS is in charge of most UK hospitals.

c *The* is used for ordinal numbers:
This is **the second operation** that she has had.

d *The* is used with superlative adjectives:
Heart disease is **the most common** health problem in our society.

Indefinite article (*a*/*an*)

e The indefinite articles *a* and *an* are used to introduce single, countable nouns which are not specified:
A doctor spoke to her patient about **an important health risk**.

Spelling

If the noun starts with a consonant, we use **a**. If the noun starts with a vowel sound, we use **an**:
A good healthcare system is **an important factor** for citizens' health.

If the noun starts with a vowel but has a consonant sound, we use **a**:
She works at **a university hospital**.

Zero article (Ø)

f No articles are needed for uncountable nouns when talking about things in general:
Water and **oxygen** are vital for **life**.

g No articles are needed for plural countable nouns when talking about things or people in general:
Nurses generally work hard.

h No articles are needed for some proper nouns such as the names of most countries or people:
Doctor Ahmadi is from **Jordan**.

GRAMMAR

Articles in discourse

i When you begin an academic essay or paragraph, it is common to start with a generalization. Use *a/an* for singular nouns and zero article for uncountable and plural nouns:

__A healthy diet__ is the key to long life.

__Good health__ is important for everyone.

j If you refer to a specific noun that is familiar to your reader, use *the*:

People with that disease know that __the drugs__ are cheaper abroad than they are here. (The reader understands which drugs are referred to by the context.)

1 Read the sentences (1–11). Decide which rule (a–j) from the box on page 73 and the box above the underlined words follow.

1 You should usually take medicine after meals. ______
2 It was the worst epidemic in many years. ______
3 It comes from India. ______
4 The British Medical Association is very well respected. ______
5 Old people are more likely to need medication than younger people. ______
6 The first time you visit your doctor, you will need to register. ______
7 A doctor and a homeopath were arguing about their theories. ______
8 It is the third most commonly prescribed medication. ______
9 Private healthcare can be very expensive. ______
10 A proper medical diagnosis should be made by a doctor. ______
11 He needs to go through chemotherapy. The treatment plan is very harsh. ______

2 Complete the sentences with *a*, *an*, *the* or zero article (Ø).

1 When travelling, it's usually easier to carry ____________ pills than ____________ bottle of medicine.
2 ____________ alternative medicine is popular in ____________ China.
3 ____________ first time I was in hospital was 2010.
4 ____________ best facility in the city is ____________ Royal Hospital.
5 In some countries, ____________ medical care is expensive.
6 It can be argued that ____________ homeopathy does no harm as ____________ additional treatment.
7 ____________ cost effectiveness is ____________ important issue in healthcare.
8 In addition, ____________ homeopathy is ____________ ancient system of ____________ medicine.
9 Medicine can be sold in a shop or prescribed by a doctor, but ____________ kind of medicine that is sold in shops is usually cheaper.
10 If you ask ____________ people what is most important to them, many of them will answer ____________ 'good health'.

TRANSITIONS TO SHOW CONCESSION

GRAMMAR

When you present an argument in writing, you often need to mention opposing arguments. You can introduce opposing views by joining sentences or clauses with certain phrases which show that there is a difference of opinion.

Homeopathy seems to be ineffective. **Other people claim that** it works.

Simple language of concession followed by a clause or a sentence:

Homeopathy seems to be ineffective, **but** some people claim that it works.
Homeopathy seems to be ineffective. **However**, some people claim that it works.

More complex language of concession

Followed by a clause: Homeopathy seems to be ineffective. **Nevertheless**, people still use it.

Even though / **Despite the fact that** / **In spite of the fact that** homeopathy seems to be ineffective, people still use it.

Followed by a noun phrase: **Despite** / **In spite of** its ineffectiveness, people still use it.

3 Complete each sentence using one of the concession words or phrases.

1 People who need expensive medicines are often willing to pay a lot of money for them, ____________ the cost.
2 ____________ the results are not scientifically proven, my mother uses this homeopathic remedy.
3 While some people say that there is no cure for the common cold, ____________ vitamins can help.
4 Government-provided healthcare is free for citizens. ____________, they do have to pay taxes to support it.
5 ____________ I am feeling very ill, I am not going to the hospital.

ACADEMIC WRITING SKILLS

SENTENCE VARIETY

SKILLS

Your academic writing will be stronger if you can vary the types of sentences that you write. You can combine longer, more complex sentences with shorter, more straightforward ones to create a text which is more interesting and has a stronger overall flow. For example, you can begin a sentence with a subordinate clause such as 'Although it is expensive, ...', or with a prepositional phrase such as 'In some countries, ... '. Notice the difference between these two texts:

A Many people do not have access to healthcare. This may be because their country's government does not provide it. It could also be because they cannot afford it. This is a problem.

All of the sentences start with a subject (e.g. 'Many people'), then have a verb (e.g. 'have'). Compare this sentence:

B Because their government does not provide it, or because it is too expensive, many people do not have healthcare. This is a problem.

Text B comes across as better writing and has a better flow. The sentences do not all follow the 'subject + verb' structure, and the first sentence here begins with a subordinate clause. Now look at these two texts.

C The healthcare system in my country is not ideal. It works adequately for the rich and the poor. It does not work adequately for middle-class citizens. This is unacceptable.

D In my country, the healthcare system, which works adequately for the rich and the poor, does not work well for middle-class citizens. This is unacceptable.

Text D uses sentence variety: starting the sentence with a preposition, and using relative clauses to combine information.

Notice the five techniques used in the examples above:

- Varying the length of sentences in a text
- Beginning sentences with subordinate clauses
- Using conjunctions to make compound sentences
- Beginning sentences with prepositions
- Using relative clauses to combine information

1 Follow the instructions to write sentences with the words provided.

1 Write two sentences: a longer one, and then a shorter one.
People / should / not / take / medicine / prescribed / someone / else / is / dangerous
People should not take medicine that is prescribed for someone else. This is dangerous.

2 Write a sentence that begins with a subordinate clause.
Although / my / country's / healthcare / system / not / perfect / better / than / many / others

3 Write a sentence that contains a relative clause.
This / medication / that / I / need / take / for / my / illness

4 Write two sentences: a longer one, and then a shorter one.
All / people / our / society / access / affordable / healthcare / their / right

5 Write a sentence that begins with a preposition.
On / this / subject / doctors / agree / most

6 Write a sentence which uses a conjunction.
A / good / healthcare / system / can / save / money / and / also / save / lives

PLUS

WRITING TASK

Is disease prevention the responsibility of individuals and their families, or of the government?

PLAN

1 Look back at your ideas in Critical thinking. Use your ideas to create an essay outline using the structure below.

Paragraph 1:	Introductory paragraph
Paragraph 2:	Argument 1 (supporting evidence / concession / solution)
Paragraph 3:	Argument 2 (supporting evidence / concession / solution)
Paragraph 4:	Concluding paragraph

2 Refer to the Task checklist on page 78 as you prepare your essay.

WRITE A FIRST DRAFT

3 Write your essay using the outline. Write 350–400 words.

REVISE

4 Use the Task checklist to review your essay for content and structure.

TASK CHECKLIST	✔
Did you give your opinion in your writing and make it clear what your response to the question is in the introduction?	
Did you use sentence variety?	
Did you mention opposing ideas?	

5 Make any necessary changes to your essay.

EDIT

6 Use the Language checklist to edit your essay for language errors.

LANGUAGE CHECKLIST	✔
Did you use articles (*the*, *a/an*, zero article) correctly?	
Did you use transitions for concession (*despite*, *although*, *however*, etc.) to show opposing views to your own arguments?	
Did you use an appropriate range of medical and academic vocabulary?	
Did you use the adjective forms of academic nouns?	

7 Make any necessary changes to your essay.

OBJECTIVES REVIEW

1 Check your learning objectives for this unit. Write *3*, *2* or *1* for each objective.

3 = very well 2 = well 1 = not so well

I can …

watch and understand a video about robots used in surgery.	_____
annotate a text.	_____
evaluate ideas.	_____
use articles.	_____
use transitions to show concession.	_____
use sentence variety.	_____
write an opinion essay.	_____

2 Use the *Unlock* Digital Workbook for more practice with this unit's learning objectives.

UNLOCK ONLINE

WORDLIST

adequate (adj) ⊙	epidemic (n) ⊙	proponent (n)
adverse (adj) ⊙	fund (v) ⊙	regardless (adv) ⊙
burden (n) ⊙	illegal (adj) ⊙	safety net (n phr)
chief (adj) ⊙	labour (n) ⊙	sedentary lifestyle (n phr)
complex (adj) ⊙	medical (adj) ⊙	substances (n) ⊙
consultation (n) ⊙	patent (n) ⊙	surgery (n) ⊙
contribution (n) ⊙	physical (adj) ⊙	symptoms (n) ⊙
controversial (adj) ⊙	precise (adj) ⊙	treatment (n) ⊙
conventional (adj) ⊙	preventable illness (n phr)	underfunding (n)
drug dependency (n phr)	professional (adj) ⊙	

⊙ = high-frequency words in the Cambridge Academic Corpus

LEARNING OBJECTIVES	IN THIS UNIT YOU WILL ...
Watch and listen	watch and understand a video about population and water.
Reading skill	identify cohesive devices.
Critical thinking	analyze a case study; evaluate arguments.
Grammar	express solutions using *it*.
Academic writing skills	develop ideas; use parallel structure.
Writing task	write a problem-solution essay.

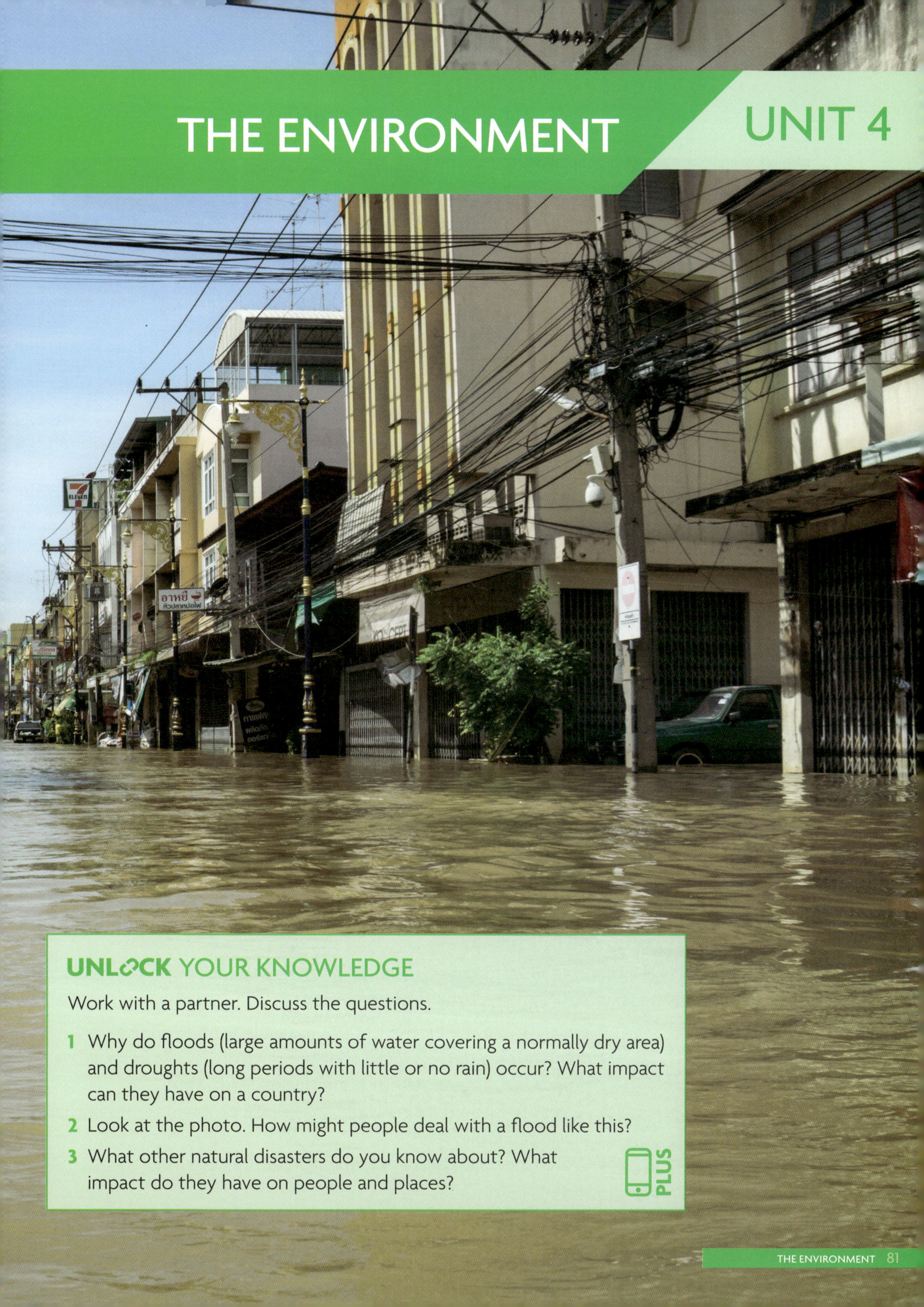

THE ENVIRONMENT

UNIT 4

UNLOCK YOUR KNOWLEDGE

Work with a partner. Discuss the questions.

1 Why do floods (large amounts of water covering a normally dry area) and droughts (long periods with little or no rain) occur? What impact can they have on a country?

2 Look at the photo. How might people deal with a flood like this?

3 What other natural disasters do you know about? What impact do they have on people and places?

PLUS

WATCH AND LISTEN

PREPARING TO WATCH

ACTIVATING YOUR KNOWLEDGE

1 Tick (✔) the statements that you agree with. Compare your answers with a partner.

1 ☐ There is an unlimited amount of clean drinking water on our planet.
2 ☐ We are losing precious natural resources.
3 ☐ Scientists are developing new ways to clean water.
4 ☐ Desert areas are the only areas in need of more water.
5 ☐ As the population grows, problems with access to clean water increase.
6 ☐ Clean water is used in the production of many goods.

PREDICTING CONTENT USING VISUALS

2 Look at the pictures from the video. Discuss the questions with your partner.

1 How much of the Earth's surface is water?
2 What parts of the world do you think are experiencing a water shortage?
3 What factors lead to water shortages?

GLOSSARY

polar ice cap (n) a thick layer of ice near the North or South Pole which permanently covers an area of land

distribution (n) the way something is divided and shared in a group or area

transform (v) to change something completely, often to improve it

reservoir (n) a natural or artificial lake for storing and supplying water for an area

WHILE WATCHING

UNDERSTANDING MAIN IDEAS

3 Watch the video. Write *T* (true), *F* (false) or *DNS* (does not say) next to the statements. Correct the false statements.

_____ 1 Only 2.5% of the Earth's water is available for human use.
_____ 2 Transforming deserts, producing energy from rivers and building cities requires over half of our available fresh water.
_____ 3 Access to clean drinking water is a critical problem for more than a billion people.
_____ 4 Water shortages are simply the result of people living in desert areas.
_____ 5 The Aral Sea now covers 25,000 square miles.

4 Watch again. Complete the summary.

SUMMARIZING

Water covers about (1)__________ of the Earth's surface. However, only a small fraction of this water is suitable for human use. While there is no more water on the planet than there was in the distant past, the (2)__________ of water has changed. This is partly due to an increase in (3)__________ ; as the number of people on the planet grows, so does the water crisis. Several factors contribute to the shortage: poor (4)__________ , politics, poverty and simply living in a dry part of the world. Cities like Mexico City are especially at risk. Shops which sell water are becoming increasingly (5)__________ . Changes in the Earth's water distribution can be seen from (6)__________ . Places like the Aral Sea and Lake Chad in the Sahara Desert have visibly changed due to (7)__________ and overuse.

MAKING INFERENCES

5 Work with a partner. Discuss the questions. Give reasons to support your answers.

1 Why do you think only a small fraction of the Earth's water is available for human use?
2 What can be done to preserve and protect fresh water?
3 How does education help in conserving water?
4 Is it important for governments to regulate water distribution and use in agriculture and manufacturing?

DISCUSSION

6 Discuss the questions with your partner. Compare your answers with another pair.

1 Have you ever observed any changes in water access in your city or country? Describe the change.
2 How often do you purchase bottles of water? How common are bottles of water today? Do they present any environmental or economic concerns?
3 What are some steps being taken now to conserve water?

READING

READING 1

PREPARING TO READ

UNDERSTANDING KEY VOCABULARY

1 Read the two paragraphs and write the correct form of each bold word next to the correct definition.

A Scientists have not yet **identified** which kind of storm is approaching the Caribbean. The last storm was a hurricane which had a **devastating** effect on the buildings near the beach, as many of them were destroyed. To prepare for this storm, there are several important **measures** which people in that area should take. For example, it is **crucial** to have plenty of water, some torches and batteries.

1 ___________ (n) a method for dealing with a situation
2 ___________ (v) to recognize something and say what that thing is
3 ___________ (adj) extremely important or necessary
4 ___________ (adj) causing a lot of damage or destruction

B Our **community** is located by the ocean and contains about 75 families. We are all working towards a **reduction** in the damage done by storms here. Part of that includes sharing the **maintenance** costs of planting sea grass and building sand fences. In the past, some families were **criticized** for not contributing their fair share of these maintenance costs.

5 ___________ (n) the people living in one particular area
6 ___________ (n) the work needed to keep something in good condition
7 ___________ (n) the act of making something smaller in size or amount
8 ___________ (v) to express disapproval of someone or something

PREDICTING CONTENT USING VISUALS

2 Look at the photos of different natural disasters and ways to prevent damage from natural disasters. Label the photos with the words from the box.

dam	flood barrier	~~levee~~	hurricane	sandbagging	tsunami

1 levee

2 ______________________

3 ______________________

4 ______________________

5 ______________________

6 ______________________

SKIMMING

3 Skim the interview with a disaster-mitigation expert. Which title below is best for the interview? Why?

1 Controlling the flow
2 What to do about risk
3 A way to protect people from flooding
4 Protect your house against flooding

1 *The world has always had to face water-based natural disasters such as tsunamis and hurricanes. In an illuminating[1] interview, Water Management Monthly talks to Dan Smith, who works in disaster mitigation for a government agency.*

2 'Dan, could you tell us what *disaster mitigation* means?'

'Disaster mitigation means attempting to minimize the impact of natural disasters both before and after they happen. My department and I work in two specific areas to try and do this: risk **reduction** and risk analysis. Both are **crucial** in disaster mitigation.'

3 'What do you mean by *risk reduction*?'

'Risk reduction means many things. It is not just referring to big engineering projects like dams. Often, small **community** projects can be the most effective means of risk reduction. The main way floods can be prevented is by the construction and **maintenance** of earth-wall defences, called levees. These block the progress of rising water. However, even the best levees can't protect against the **devastating** power of a tsunami. In this case, early-warning systems are lifesavers. They can let people know as early as possible if there is likely to be flooding.'

4 'What types of risk analysis do you do?'

'Firstly, risk analysis concerns flood mapping, where we **identify** the parts of the country which are at most risk from flooding. Secondly, there is mitigation planning, which helps local communities plan for when disaster strikes. Thirdly, we make sure that the country's dams all work properly and are safe. Although many people **criticize** dams because of their environmental impact, they also have many benefits such as hydroelectricity, irrigation, water storage, water sports and, of course, flood control. In terms of a cost-benefit analysis, we are definitely ahead.'

5 'Do you think countries are better prepared now for natural disasters than they were in the past?'

'Definitely. We are constantly developing new flood-prevention solutions. Some examples of these kinds of **measures** include the construction of sea walls and bulkheads[2], which protect the coasts, and the redesign of power stations and subway tunnels in the New York City area after the devastating damage caused by Hurricane Sandy in 2012. In the UK, another good example is the Thames Barrier, a huge engineering project designed to prevent London from flooding.'

6 'Aren't programmes like that very expensive? What lower-cost alternatives are there?'

'Flood prevention does not have to be expensive. Sandbags, for example, can be a highly effective way of stopping flood water.'

7 'Is there any more that can be done, or are we as prepared as we can be?'

'There's always more that could be done. But remember that the government can only be responsible for flood prevention up to a certain point. People have to become aware of the dangers of flooding themselves. This is crucial. Expensive early-warning systems are a waste of money if people pay no attention to them.'

[1]**illuminating** (adj) giving you new information about a subject
[2]**bulkhead** (n) an underwater wall

WHILE READING

READING FOR DETAIL

4 Read the interview again. Write *T* (true), *F* (false) or *DNS* (does not say) next to the statements. Correct the false statements.

_____ 1 Dan Smith works for an international organization.
_____ 2 Risk reduction and risk analysis are both important parts of disaster mitigation.
_____ 3 Large-scale projects are always effective for risk reduction.
_____ 4 Planning for natural disasters has improved in recent years.
_____ 5 The New York City subway tunnel redesign cost $20 million.
_____ 6 Low-technology solutions can protect against flooding, too.

5 Answer the following questions based on the text.

1 What is the function of *disaster mitigation*?
2 What is a synonym phrase for a *levee*?
3 Why do some people criticize dams?
4 Who is responsible for flood prevention?

SKILLS

Identifying cohesive devices

Good academic writing flows easily and is not too repetitive. The writer needs to show links between ideas without repeating the same words. Using pronouns and synonyms in the place of nouns and noun phrases can help. To read well in English, you need to be able to identify what these pronouns and synonyms refer to.

Droughts often occur in central Kenya. **This area** is so dry that it cannot support crops.

In order to avoid repetition, the writer refers back to central Kenya with a pronoun in a new noun phrase: '*this* area'.

Droughts can also cause people to suffer if the **lack of water** means that people don't have enough to drink.

Here, the writer refers back to the idea of droughts with a synonym phrase: 'lack of water'.

6 Find these words and phrases underlined in the interview. Write the nouns or noun phrases that they refer to.

1 two specific areas _______________
2 It _______________
3 These _______________
4 this case _______________
5 these kinds of measures _______________
6 that _______________
7 them _______________

READING BETWEEN THE LINES

MAKING INFERENCES

7 Work with a partner. Which of the opinions do you think Dan Smith would agree with?

1 It's the government's responsibility to protect us from natural disasters.
2 Surely it's more important to spend time and money on ways to stop water from causing floods, rather than finding out which areas are likely to flood. We already know that.
3 Dams are more trouble than they're worth.
4 Building sea walls is a waste of money – sandbags are just as good.
5 People in flood-risk areas need to be educated about the risks and about how they can help themselves.

DISCUSSION

8 Work with a partner. Discuss the questions.

1 How would life in your country be different if you had higher or lower rainfall?
2 Does your country ever have problems with flooding? If so, how do people protect themselves?
3 Which countries have particularly serious problems with flooding? Can you think of reasons why?

READING 2

PREPARING TO READ

UNDERSTANDING KEY VOCABULARY

1 You are going to read an article on droughts in rural Africa. Read the definitions. Complete the sentences with the correct form of the words in bold.

casualty (n) a person hurt or killed in a serious accident or event
disrupt (v) to prevent something from continuing as expected
infrastructure (n) the basic systems and services, such as transport and power, that a country uses to work effectively
issue (n) a subject or problem which people are thinking about or discussing
monitor (v) to watch and check something carefully over a period of time
policy (n) a set of ideas or a plan for action that a business, government, political party or group of people follow
rely on (phr v) to depend on or trust someone or something
strategy (n) a long-range plan for achieving a goal

1 A hurricane ________ our holiday to the Caribbean, and we had to return home sooner than expected.
2 The local government was relieved that there were no ________ in the earthquake. Everyone was safe.
3 There are several effective ________ for preventing coastal damage from high waves and flood water, such as planting sea grass, using sandbags and constructing sea walls and bulkheads.
4 Environmental pollution is a(n) ________ that more people are paying attention to. There is more recycling and less use of plastic.
5 Companies are now asked to ________ their greenhouse gas emissions to make sure they are not too high.
6 Some environmentalists don't think we should just ________ the government to regulate pollution. They believe we need citizens to be involved as well.
7 Developing countries often lack a strong enough ________ to be able to provide water and electricity to all residents.
8 The Environmental Protection Agency's ________ is to make sure that the government considers the environmental effects of its plans.

PLUS

PREDICTING CONTENT USING VISUALS

2 Drought is a major problem in many parts of the world. Look at the map and identify areas where you think drought may be common.

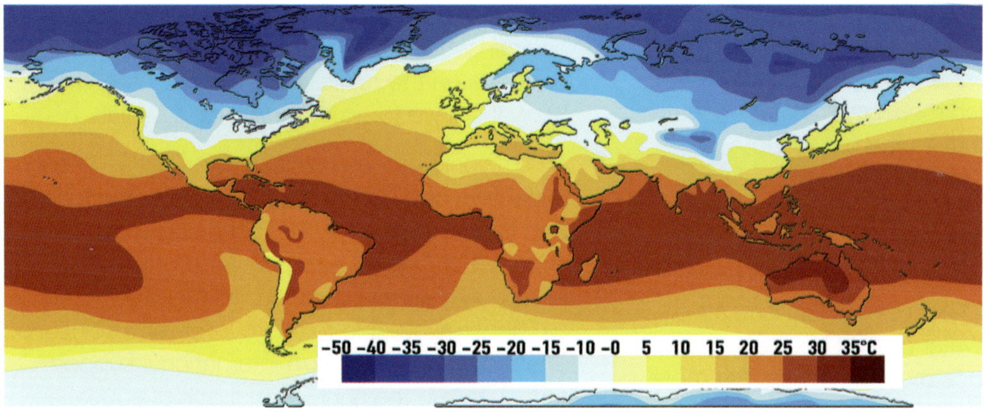

Average world temperatures

USING YOUR KNOWLEDGE

3 Work with a partner. Discuss the questions.
1 What are the effects of drought?
2 How can people suffering from drought be helped in the short term?
3 What are some long-term solutions to a shortage of water?
4 Why do developing countries in particular struggle with droughts?

Combatting drought in rural Africa

1 In order to mitigate the problems which drought can bring, there are several short- and long-term **strategies** which can be adopted. A range of **policies** designed to combat these problems exists at local, national and international levels. As well as general **issues** related to this topic, there are specific recommendations which can be made in the case of Kenya, where drought has been a major problem in recent years.

2 Droughts frequently put millions of people at risk of food insecurity[1] in central Kenya. The area is so dry that it cannot support agricultural crops. There are few permanent rivers, and the seasonal waterways caused by flood waters in the rainy months **disrupt** transport across the region. The people of this area mainly live off their cattle. Droughts can quickly kill off their animals, which eliminates their main source of income. Finally, because the area is so vast, **infrastructure** is under-developed, so access to the population is difficult.

3 When drought is predicted in central Kenya, it is important to employ short-term preventative measures and be prepared to respond to it as quickly as possible in order to minimize **casualties**. One such measure is recycling water. Recycled water, from the washing of clothes for example, can be given to animals and used to irrigate[2] land. A programme of this kind can be achieved in two to three months. To do this on a regional level in central Kenya would only cost about $100,000 per year, which is relatively cost-effective. This water cannot be drunk by people, however. Once drought strikes, the most important response is to transport bottles of drinking water into the drought area. This can be done quickly (within one week), but it is quite expensive. Kenya has 47 million people, and to import bottled water for even a quarter of the population could cost as much as $10 million per year. In addition, since drought also often kills animals and crops, it is also vital to bring food to prevent people from starving.

[1]**food insecurity** (n) the state of being without reliable access to a sufficient quantity of affordable, nutritious food
[2]**irrigate** (v) to supply land with water so that crops and plants will grow
[3]**wells** (n) deep holes in the ground which hold water

4 Drought tends to reoccur in the same central areas of Kenya, so long-term solutions are also necessary. The authorities need to **monitor** droughts and gather relevant data. As they are already being paid for their government jobs, this should not add any extra costs to the national budget. The data can then be used for appropriate planning at the local and national levels. This part costs more, as it involves developing irrigation systems for farming communities, or building canals and dams to benefit villages and cities. This could cost as much as $8 million and take as long as two years. On a micro-scale, the construction of wells[3] can help provide more water at a cost of about $500,000. Once the funding is in place, this can be done immediately. On a wider scale, desalination plants, which remove salt from sea water, also make drinking water available, but at a much higher cost of about seven to ten million dollars. These plants can take years to construct before they are running efficiently – perhaps as long as five years. Additionally, harvesting rainwater lets communities collect and store any rain which does fall. This is less costly, but it depends on the rainfall in the area. Sometimes Kenyans have to wait months for a rainfall.

5 The majority of these strategies are undoubtedly expensive and may only be affordable for richer countries, which have the technology and expertise to predict and plan for drought more effectively. Poorer countries, on the other hand, are generally unable to afford long-term solutions, and may have to **rely on** international support and charity in the short term. Lack of education and under-developed infrastructure may also hamper some of these projects.

6 Overall, we can see that there are several recommendations that can be made for Kenya's drought problems. First, the provision of training in recycling and harvesting water throughout the country at a local level. Second, the implementation of a well-construction programme to maximize the amount of water available nationally. Third, a movement to lobby the international community to provide funding for a desalination plant on the coast to ensure that Kenya can always meet its water needs.

WHILE READING

READING FOR MAIN IDEAS

4 Read the article. Write the corresponding paragraph number next to the purpose mentioned in the article.

a sets out a number of suggestions ______
b considers economic factors in decision-making ______
c introduces the main purpose of the text ______
d discusses a range of long-term strategies ______
e discusses a range of short-term strategies ______
f briefs the reader on the effects of drought in Kenya ______

READING FOR DETAIL

5 Read the article again. Place the strategies for dealing with drought in the appropriate places in the diagram.

1 constructing dams
2 rainwater harvesting
3 building wells
4 bringing in drinking water
5 water recycling
6 constructing desalination plants

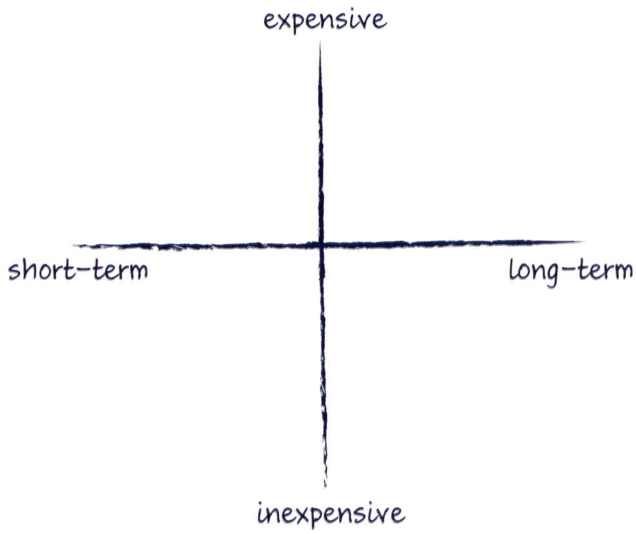

READING BETWEEN THE LINES

MAKING INFERENCES

6 Choose the best answers.

1 What aspect of this issue does the writer feel is important to understand?
   a the moral challenges of dealing with drought
   b the financial aspects of dealing with drought
2 Why are the people of central Kenya most at risk of drought?
   a their way of life means they need to use a lot of water
   b the area experiences low annual rainfall
3 Which of these points do you think the author agrees with most?
   a Partnership between organizations is important in preventing drought.
   b Every country should follow the recommendations in this article.

DISCUSSION

SYNTHESIZING

7 Work with a partner. Use ideas from Reading 1 and Reading 2 to discuss the questions.

1 Has your country ever experienced drought?
2 Which strategies mentioned in the text does your country use?
3 Which do you think would be more difficult to live through: a severe drought, or a severe flood? Why?

PLUS

LANGUAGE DEVELOPMENT

ACADEMIC NOUN PHRASES

VOCABULARY

Two or three nouns may sometimes be combined in academic writing in order to create a more complex noun phrase which gives greater detail about the subject.

risk + analysis = risk analysis
risk + analysis + project = risk analysis project

The meaning of the more complex noun phrase will contain elements of the base nouns.

risk = danger, threat
analysis = the process of looking at something in detail
project = a piece of work with a particular focus
risk analysis = the process of looking at dangers or threats in detail
risk analysis project = a piece of work which looks at dangers or threats in detail

When creating noun phrases, it may be necessary to make a noun out of adjectives, verbs or adverbs (i.e., to *nominalize* them).

manufacture the product = product manufacturing

1 Complete each sentence (b) with an academic noun phrase formed from words in each sentence (a).

1 a We need to mitigate these kinds of disasters.
  b We need disaster mitigation.
2 a An important component of managing natural disasters is reducing risk.
  b ______________ is an important component of managing natural disasters.
3 a It is important for a country to have a system for managing water to protect against flooding.
  b It is important for a country to have a ______________ to protect against flooding.
4 a The report made by the government was very influential.
  b The ______________ was very influential.

5 a The need for protection against floods is particularly relevant in towns located near rivers.
   b The need for ____________________ is particularly relevant in towns located near rivers.
6 a Projects based in the community can be effective in minimizing risk.
   b ____________________ can be effective in minimizing risk.

NATURAL DISASTER VOCABULARY

2 Look at the adjective-noun collocations. Circle the collocation in each group which has a different meaning.

1 A *huge* / *enormous* / *minor* problem.
2 *natural* / *terrible* / *major* disaster
3 *severe* / *devastating* / *controlled* flood
4 *wide-reaching* / *large-scale* / *long-term* disaster mitigation project
5 *serious* / *seasonal* / *extreme* drought

3 Complete the sentences with collocations from Exercise 2. In some cases, more than one answer may be possible.

1 Owing to their complexity, desalination plants are long-term projects, which may take many years to construct.
2 One of the worst ____________________ in human history was the 1556 earthquake in Shaanxi Province, China.
3 ____________________ are sometimes used to improve the quality of rivers.
4 ____________________ such as dams, flood defences and early warning systems require huge amounts of investment.
5 In 1931, there was a(n) ____________________ in China, where more than a million people lost their lives to the water.
6 Because of a very hot climate, sub-Saharan Africa suffers from ____________________ more than many other places in the world.
7 In an increasing number of places, the lack of winter rain makes the chances of ____________________ in the summer more likely.
8 Where proper planning has been in place, the chances of a flood or drought turning into a ____________________ are reduced.

PLUS

PLUS

WRITING

CRITICAL THINKING

At the end of this unit, you are going to write a problem–solution essay. Look at this unit's writing task below.

> Write an essay which provides both short- and long-term solutions to an environmental problem and takes the costs into consideration. Refer to a specific case study in your essay.

ANALYZE

1 Read the two case studies. Match strategies (1–9) to case studies (A–B). Each strategy may be applied to one or both case studies.

Case study A: Wildfire risk

Location: Southern Australia
Geography: heavily forested areas
Country GDP rank in world: #12
Potential causes of fire: drought, arson[1], global warming
Human consequences: 1–5 deaths per year
Frequency: common during summer months
Effects: loss of life, destruction of homes and other buildings; destruction of habitats for wild animals; pollution from smoke
Short-term solutions: better law enforcement against arson, establishing volunteer fire groups (£0 per year); using satellite images and drone aircrafts to detect and follow fires (£15,000 per year)
Long-term solution: Government restrictions against building in hot, dry areas (£0 per year)

[1]**arson** (n) the crime of intentionally starting a fire in order to damage or destroy something

Case study B: Dust storms

Location: Mauritania, North Africa
Geography: mainly desert
Country GDP rank in world: #154
Potential causes: wind, drought, farming practices, deforestation
Human consequences: difficult to measure, as fatal consequences are not always immediate
Frequency: until early 1960s about two per year; since 1960s, 80 per year
Effects: loss of fertile soil; health dangers (breathing problems); poor visibility for transport
Short-term solutions: force better farming practices in the country such as crop rotation (£0 per year); stop deforestation (national income loss approx. £25,000 per year)
Long-term solutions: improved national irrigation systems (£500,000 per year); set up more clinics to treat people with asthma and other health problems (£7 million per year)

	strategies	case studies
1	Stopping deforestation	________
2	Educating the community about prevention and protection	________
3	Setting up more clinics to treat sick people	________
4	Increasing law enforcement against arson	________
5	Establishing volunteer groups	________
6	Improving irrigation systems	________
7	Restricting the areas where building is allowed	________
8	Encouraging responsible farming practices	________
9	Developing monitoring systems via satellites and drones	________

SKILLS

Evaluating arguments

When you need to evaluate arguments against two different criteria simultaneously, a diagram like the one below and on page 91 is a very effective tool. At each end of the x-axis and the y-axis, add opposing factors. Then place the argument at the relevant point (e.g. in the top-right section if expensive and long-term; in the bottom-left if inexpensive and short-term).

2 Now read the case studies again and place the preventive strategies from Exercise 1 in the diagram.

EVALUATE

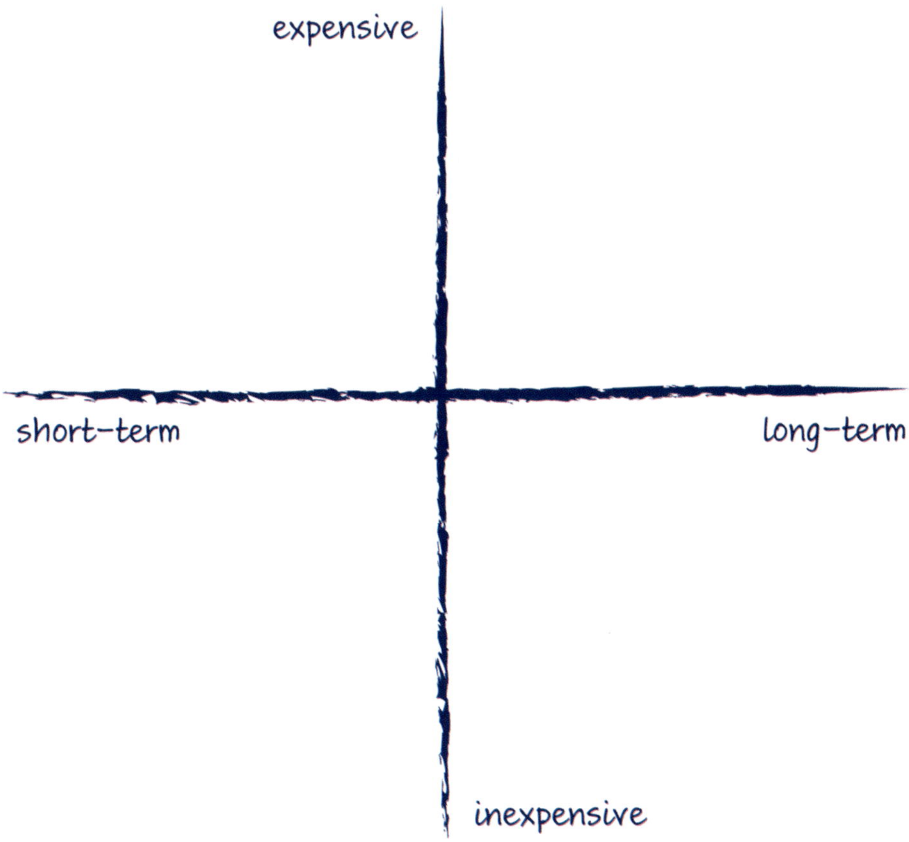

3 Answer the following questions. Assume that there is a developing country which sometimes has wildfires or dust storms, but which is not currently following any of the strategies mentioned in the case studies.

1 Which measures would be easiest to take? Which would be hardest?

____

____

2 Can you think of any other measures not mentioned in the case studies?

____

____

3 Choose the three best solutions to recommend to each country.

____

____

4 Compare your answers with a partner. Make any changes to your answers in Exercise 3 based on any good suggestions you hear.

GRAMMAR FOR WRITING

EXPRESSING SOLUTIONS USING *IT*

GRAMMAR

Most sentences in English need a subject as well as a verb.

Minimizing the risks caused by natural disasters is possible.

The words in bold are the subject. When the subject is long like this, it sounds better to change the sentence, so we use *it* as the subject.

It is possible to minimize the risks caused by natural disasters.

Note that *it* has no meaning in this structure. *It* does not refer to anything else in the text. *It* is only included to provide a subject for the sentence.

There are a number of grammar patterns which follow *it*.

1 *it* + *is* + noun phrase or adjective + infinitive
It is a good idea to keep an emergency kit at home.
It is important to prepare for natural disasters.

2 *it* + *is* + adjective + gerund
It is worth preparing for natural disasters.

3 *it* + *is* + noun phrase or adjective + *that* + clause
It is surprising that governments do not always prepare for disasters.
It is a sad fact that many lives were lost.

1 The sentence halves in the first column are commonly used phrases in writing. Match the sentence halves. In some cases, more than one answer may be possible.

1 It is important
2 It is unlikely
3 It can be difficult
4 It is worth
5 It is not worth
6 It is never a good idea to
7 It is not surprising
8 It is not easy to

a preparing for droughts even during the rainy season.
b to protect homes and businesses from floods.
c to guarantee flood protection in areas close to major rivers.
d that a tsunami can overcome large-scale flood defences.
e build homes in a flood zone.
f that short-term drought solutions will work over a long period.
g persuade people to move away from areas at risk of floods.
h investing in tsunami warnings if people don't pay attention to them.

2 Complete the sentences with your own ideas.

1 It is important to prepare for a flood by ______________________
______________________.
2 It is never a good idea to build houses ______________________
______________________.
3 In areas that suffer from drought, it's worth ______________________
______________________.
4 When working with many different organizations, it can be difficult
____
______________________.
5 Given how complex dam-construction projects are, it is not surprising
____
______________________.
6 After a serious natural disaster, it is not easy to ______________________
______________________.

3 Now choose three of the phrases with *it* from Exercises 1 or 2, and write your own sentences.

Example: It is important *to help other countries when they experience natural disasters.*
____
____
____

4 Share your answers with a partner, and discuss your ideas.

ACADEMIC WRITING SKILLS

DEVELOPING IDEAS

SKILLS

A body paragraph which supports a thesis statement must give reasons why the thesis is valid by providing examples. These examples need to be sequenced in a logical way. The presentation of ideas in a body paragraph needs to be cohesive – it needs to 'flow' well, and the connection of ideas should be clear to the reader. End a body paragraph with a sentence that gives the idea a 'finished' feeling.

1 Number the sentences to create a body paragraph that flows logically. Then re-write the paragraph in the correct order.

- **a** Another way is to harvest rainwater by collecting and storing any that does fall and using it for flushing toilets and watering gardens. ____
- **b** In very dry regions of the world, it is important to conserve as much water as possible. ____
- **c** The first step to take is to avoid wasting water by making sure taps are completely turned off after use. ____
- **d** These measures can all be very effective in saving water. ____
- **e** The water from the shower, sink and washing machine can also be used for these purposes. ____
- **f** This is the cheapest and easiest way to ensure inhabitants have adequate water for their everyday needs. ____

PARALLEL STRUCTURE

SKILLS

When you write a list of words or phrases connected with conjunctions such as *and*, they should either be the same part of speech or they should all be clauses. This is called *parallel structure*.

The government needs to <u>monitor hurricane activity</u> (verb phrase) and <u>alert the public</u> (verb phrase).

Floods and droughts can be <u>dangerous</u> (adjective), <u>damaging</u> (adjective) and <u>costly</u> (adjective).

To minimize casualties in natural disasters, <u>the government should be prepared</u> (clause) and <u>people need to be warned</u> (clause).

If you do not use the same part of speech, the writing 'violates' parallel structure. This is not good writing.

Environmental problems that people are concerned about include <u>air pollution</u> (noun phrase), <u>lack of safe water</u> (noun phrase) and ~~they worry about global warming~~ (clause).
^ global warming

PLUS

2 Read the sentences. Correct the words or phrases which do not have parallel structure.

1 People can learn about approaching storms from the regular media, social media sites, or talk to their friends and neighbours.
2 In places like Kenya, residents can prepare for droughts by recycling water, building wells and they should establish desalination plants.
3 Dan Smith is a specialist in disaster mitigation, risk reduction and he analyzes risk.
4 Severe storms can be very scary, seriously damaging and the expense is surprising.
5 Common examples of natural disasters include earthquakes, floods and typhoons can also occur.

3 Finish these sentences with an appropriate parallel structure phrase.

1 We should keep many things in our homes to stay safe during a storm, such as bottled water, ________________________ .
2 When a tsunami occurs, it can damage buildings and ________________________ .
3 There are several strategies that Australia can use to prepare for wildfires, such as monitoring the area with drones, ________________________ .

WRITING TASK

Write an essay which provides both short- and long-term solutions to an environmental problem and takes the costs into consideration. Refer to a specific case study in your essay.

PLAN

1 Look back at your notes about the case study you chose and the diagram in Critical thinking. Create an outline for your essay using this structure.

> 1 Introductory paragraph: description of the problem and main purpose of report
> 2 Recommended solution #1
> 3 Recommended solution #2
> 4 Recommended solution #3
> 5 Concluding paragraph: summary and evaluation of key points

2 Refer to the Task checklist on page 100 as you prepare your essay.

WRITE A FIRST DRAFT

3 Complete the essay using your outline. Write 350–400 words.

REVISE

4 Use the Task checklist to review your essay for content and structure.

TASK CHECKLIST	✔
Did you use an appropriate structure for the essay?	
Do your paragraphs all include topic sentences and the development of ideas?	
Did you identify both short- and long-term solutions in your essay?	
Did you include relevant supporting information in the essay?	
Did you make sure all of your sentences contain parallel structure?	
Did you refer to a case study?	

5 Make any necessary changes to your essay.

EDIT

6 Use the Language checklist to edit your essay for language errors.

LANGUAGE CHECKLIST	✔
Did you use academic noun phrases where appropriate?	
Did you check that the words in your phrases collocate correctly?	
Did you correctly use phrases with *it*, where appropriate?	
Did you spell any environmental collocations correctly?	

7 Make any necessary changes to your essay.

OBJECTIVES REVIEW

1 Check your learning objectives for this unit. Write *3*, *2* or *1* for each objective.

3 = very well   2 = well   1 = not so well

I can …

watch and understand a video about population and water.	_____
identify cohesive devices.	_____
analyze a case study.	_____
evaluate arguments.	_____
express solutions using *it*.	_____
develop ideas.	_____
use parallel structure.	_____
write a problem-solution essay.	_____

2 Use the *Unlock* Digital Workbook for more practice with this unit's learning objectives.

UNLOCK ONLINE

WORDLIST

casualty (n)
community (n) ⊙
criticize (v)
crucial (adj) ⊙
devastating (adj)
disaster (n) ⊙
disrupt (v)
extreme (adj) ⊙
identify (v) ⊙
infrastructure (n) ⊙
issue (n) ⊙
large-scale (adj) ⊙
long-term (adj) ⊙
maintenance (n) ⊙
major (adj) ⊙
measure (n) ⊙
monitor (v) ⊙
policy (n) ⊙
reduction (n) ⊙
rely on (phr v)
severe (adj) ⊙
strategy (n) ⊙

⊙ = high-frequency words in the Cambridge Academic Corpus

LEARNING OBJECTIVES	IN THIS UNIT YOU WILL ...
Watch and listen	watch and understand a video about government grants for energy-efficient homes.
Reading skill	skim a text.
Critical thinking	create a persuasive argument.
Grammar	use correct register in academic writing.
Academic writing skills	order information; prioritize arguments.
Writing task	write a persuasive essay.

ARCHITECTURE

UNLOCK YOUR KNOWLEDGE

Work with a partner. Discuss the questions.

1 Do people in your country generally live in houses or apartments?

2 What is the most important room in your home? Why?

3 What would you change about your home, school or workplace to improve it?

4 Are there any famous old buildings in your country? Are they protected? Do you think this is important? Why / Why not?

PLUS

WATCH AND LISTEN

PREPARING TO WATCH

ACTIVATING YOUR KNOWLEDGE

1 Work with a partner and answer the questions.

1 A lot of energy is wasted in buildings. How do people waste energy in their homes?
2 How can people reduce the amount of energy they waste in their homes?
3 Can the government help reduce the amount of energy that is wasted in our homes? How?

PREDICTING CONTENT USING VISUALS

2 Look at the pictures from the video. Discuss the questions with a partner.

1 The workers in the first and second picture are making these homes more energy-efficient. How do you think they are doing that?
2 What do you notice about the house in the last picture?
3 What do you think the climate is like where these homes are? Do the homes need heat? Air conditioning?

GLOSSARY

insulation (n) covering that prevents heat, sound, or electricity from escaping
intense lobbying (n phr) a powerful effort to convince the government to do something
be a rarity (v) to be very unusual
the norm (n) the usual way that things happen
scrap (v) to not continue with a plan
set something back (phr v) to make things happen more slowly than they should

WHILE WATCHING

UNDERSTANDING MAIN IDEAS

3 Watch the video. Write *T* (true) or *F* (false) next to the statements below. Correct the false statements.

_____ 1 Most homes in Britain are not very well insulated.
_____ 2 The government helps low-income home owners with the cost of insulation.
_____ 3 Britain will reach its target of an 80% reduction in emissions by 2050.

_____ 4 Builders are struggling to work out how to build more energy-efficient homes.

_____ 5 The government no longer supports the zero-carbon home standard.

_____ 6 Housing developments with energy-efficient homes are uncommon in Britain.

UNDERSTANDING DETAIL

4 Watch again. Complete the notes.

[1]____________________ of the money that people in Britain spend on heating is wasted because their homes do not have enough [2]____________________ . The government wants to change that, aiming for an 80% [3]____________________ in emissions. Builders already know how to build [4]____________________ homes. They can build homes that maintain a comfortable [5]____________________ without using much energy. Nevertheless, the emissions rate in Britain is [6]____________________ . Earlier, there was a [7]____________________ standard for building homes, but after an intense lobbying effort, it was [8]____________________ . Today, with no clear standard, builders are [9]____________________ about what kind of homes they should build.

MAKING INFERENCES

5 Work with a partner. Discuss the questions. Give reasons for your answers.

1 The 'passive-house standard' means that houses stay warm enough without extra heating. How do you think that works?
2 Why do you think there was 'intense lobbying' against the passive-house standard? Who do you think was lobbying against it?
3 The expert in the video says that zero-emissions homes are within our grasp. Do you think Britain will reach this goal soon? Why / Why not?

DISCUSSION

6 Work with a partner and answer the questions.

1 Is the home you live in energy-efficient? Give some examples to support your answer.
2 Who makes the decisions about how homes are built (for example, how much insulation is used) in your community?
3 Is your community concerned about energy efficiency? Give some examples.
4 What are some other major sources of carbon emissions outside of homes?

READING

READING 1

PREPARING TO READ

USING YOUR KNOWLEDGE

1 You are going to read an article about 'green' buildings. Work with a partner. Answer the questions.

1 Why do some people care about buildings being environmentally friendly?
2 How can architects design buildings that use less energy?
3 How can we reduce the amount of energy we use in our homes?

UNDERSTANDING KEY VOCABULARY

2 Read the definitions. Complete the sentences with the words in bold.

compromise (n) an agreement between two sides who have different opinions, in which each side gives up something it had wanted
conservation (n) the protection of plants, animals and natural areas from the damaging effects of human activity
durable (adj) able to last a long time without being damaged
efficiency (n) the condition or fact of producing the results you want without waste
relevant (adj) related to a subject or to something happening or being discussed
second-hand (adj) not new; having been used in the past by someone else
sector (n) a part of society which can be separated from other parts because of its own special character

1 Buildings which are tough and last a long time are usually made from ________ materials.
2 The city planning committee may have to make a(n) ________ in order to both save money and use high-quality building materials.
3 It is important for developers to consider the ________ of their plan so that they avoid wasting time, money or labour.
4 Developers cannot build in certain locations, such as rainforests, due to environmental ________ .
5 If previously used wood is still in good condition, a builder may choose to use it for construction even though it is ________ .
6 Most architects work in the private ________ , which means they work for companies and not for the government.
7 The architect who designed the building does not think people's opinion of its appearance is ________ to its purpose.

SKILLS

Skimming a text

Skimming is reading a text quickly in order to get a general idea of its main points. It is particularly useful when you have a great deal of information to read in a short space of time, or when it is not necessary to understand a text in detail. Readers often skim a text to find out if it will be useful or not before reading it more thoroughly. This is particularly important in academic reading where you may only have time to read the most useful information.

Do ...

✔ look at the title, any subheadings and illustrations – they will often give clues about the content.
✔ read the introductory paragraph, which should tell you what the text will be about.
✔ read the concluding paragraph.
✔ read the first sentence of each paragraph, which may present its topic.

Don't ...

✗ stop to look up unknown words.
✗ say the individual words that you read in your head. Try to just focus on the meaning.
✗ read examples.

SKIMMING

3 Look at the photos with the article on page 108. Read only the title, the introductory paragraph and the concluding paragraph. Complete the statement below.

This article will be useful for a student who needs to find out about ...

a houses in New Mexico.
b the causes of climate change.
c the conservation of ancient buildings.
d arguments for ecologically responsible construction.

4 How did you find the answer for Exercise 3? What was most helpful – the photos, the title, the introductory paragraph or the concluding paragraph?

5 Skim the article and write the corresponding paragraph numbers next to the ideas below. Then check your answers with a partner.

a a type of eco-building ______
b a specific example of an eco-home ______
c a current trend in construction ______
d the need to produce eco-buildings ______
e the pros and cons of producing eco-buildings ______
f an example of a public eco-building ______

We need more green buildings

1 In recent years, there has been a general trend for new buildings to be more environmentally friendly, or more 'green'. Such a building is sometimes called an *eco-building*. These buildings use energy and water efficiently, which reduces waste and pollution. However, installing features like solar panels and water-recycling systems involves higher construction costs than in a traditional building. Despite these extra costs, green buildings are good for the planet and their benefits are clear.

2 In New Mexico, in the US, there are homes, called *Earthship houses*, constructed from recycled bottles, tyres, aluminium cans and other rubbish. Often the cans, bottles and tyres are filled with soil and then the outsides are covered with natural mud. These homes are designed to use solar power – the energy from the sun – rather than electricity produced from fossil fuels[1]. These recycled-construction designs are just as **relevant** for other types of buildings. In both Uruguay and Sierra Leone, for example, there are recycled-construction schools for local children.

3 In the UAE, the Zulekha Hospital in Sharjah was the first Middle Eastern building to be awarded 'platinum certification' by the Green Building Council. They received this by meeting various green requirements, including sustainability, water and energy efficiency and indoor environmental quality. The hospital executives researched ways to make the hospital green during the construction phase of the building, and numerous features were put into the design to make it sustainable and show their commitment to the environment.

4 Another example of an eco-building is a private residence in Wales known as the 'Hobbit House'. Its frame is made of wood and the walls are made of straw, which provides excellent insulation. The roof consists of mud planted with grass, which keeps heat in and has a low impact on the environment. Solar panels provide electricity for lighting and electrical equipment. Water is supplied directly from a nearby river and is also collected from the roof for use in the garden, avoiding the need to waste clean water. Low-impact houses like this one are green because they use **second-hand** materials and do not rely on fossil fuels, but instead use renewable energy sources such as solar or wind power.

5 Critics of these kinds of eco-buildings say that while they may be good for the environment, there are practical problems with their affordability. They are often too costly to become a large-volume method of construction. There are further concerns over their long-term **efficiency**. Not much energy can be realistically generated by solar panels in places which do not have large amounts of sunlight, and not every location has access to a natural water source. However, overall, green buildings are worth it. Yet, in order to finance environmentally friendly construction and produce an affordable building, **compromises** have to be made. These may be that the building will have to be smaller or made of less **durable** materials and with technology which uses more energy. Perhaps these compromises are easier to make for schools, where ideas about **conservation** are useful for education, or for businesses where ecologically aware features are a useful marketing tool, rather than for private homes.

6 The argument for constructing green buildings is clear. According to the United Nations, material resource use in the construction **sector** is expected to reach nearly 90 billion tonnes very soon, and may more than double by 2050. Without greater resource efficiency, sustainable development goals will not succeed. We need to be wise about how we use these resources for the good of the planet. However, it remains to be seen whether we are able to accept the financial and practical compromises of producing and living in environmentally friendly buildings.

[1]**fossil fuels** (n) fuels such as gas, coal and oil produced in the earth from the remains of plants and animals

WHILE READING

READING FOR DETAIL

6 Read the article. Write *RC* (recycled-construction building), *HH* (Hobbit House) or *N* (neither type of building) for the architectural features below.

1 a grass roof ______
2 a local water source ______
3 recycled cans and bottles ______
4 gas heating ______
5 a wooden construction ______
6 straw walls ______
7 recycled tyres ______
8 natural insulation ______

7 Read the article again. Write *T* (true), *F* (false) or *DNS* (does not say) next to the statements. Then correct the false statements.

______ 1 Generally, eco-buildings are becoming more popular.
______ 2 Eco-buildings cost double the price of a traditional building.
______ 3 Environmentally friendly practices are relevant, no matter what size of building you are constructing.
______ 4 Some old construction methods can be useful in environmentally friendly construction.
______ 5 Fossil fuels are examples of renewable types of energy.
______ 6 Some schools are eco-friendly buildings.
______ 7 The United Nations produces data about global energy use.

READING BETWEEN THE LINES

MAKING INFERENCES

8 Work with a partner. Answer the questions.

1 In the introduction, it is stated that 'the benefits are clear'. What do you think those benefits are?
2 Why do you think it was necessary for the Zulekha Hospital in Sharjah to consider green features during the construction phase, rather than later on?
3 How do you think recycled-construction schools might be effective educational aids for the students who attend them?

DISCUSSION

9 Work with a partner. Discuss the questions.

1 Would you live in an eco-home if you had to pay more for its environmentally friendly features? Why / Why not?
2 Do you think there should be restrictions on how much energy individuals or institutions should be allowed to use? Why / Why not?

PLUS

READING 2

PREPARING TO READ

UNDERSTANDING KEY VOCABULARY

1 You are going to read an essay on form and function in building design. Read the sentences and choose the best definition for the words in bold.

1 The **function** of an architectural drawing is to show what the building design looks like before it is built.
   a complexity or detail
   b a purpose, or the way something works
2 Buildings which have no windows and are box-like with no unique features or decoration can seem very **depressing**.
   a making you feel unhappy and without hope
   b making you feel physically weak and less active
3 When you see a magnificent work of art, such as a painting or a beautiful building, the creativity behind it can be **inspiring**.
   a giving you new ideas and making you feel you want to do something
   b informative or educational
4 I felt that the people in that city must be pretty **civilized** when I saw the beautiful parks and buildings that they have.
   a having a well-developed way of life and social systems
   b relating to legal issues
5 It **reflects** badly **on** citizens who do not take care of their public parks and buildings.
   a reacts to
   b causes people to think of someone or something in a specified way
6 That architect has a wonderful **reputation** in her field; she is widely admired by many other architects.
   a the general opinion that people have about someone
   b a collection of works
7 He **demonstrated** the new construction technique for the public at the building design convention.
   a criticized or disapproved of something
   b showed how to do something; explained

PLUS

USING YOUR KNOWLEDGE

2 Work with a partner. Discuss the questions.

1 What are the most beautiful buildings in your country?
2 Are these buildings older buildings or modern constructions?
3 Do people in your country generally prefer modern or older houses?
4 Which is more important for a building: its beauty or its function?

SKIMMING

3 Skim the essay opposite. Does the writer think it is more important to design a building which is beautiful or one which is functional?

BUILDING DESIGN: form vs function

1 At the start of the twentieth century, Louis Sullivan, one of the creators of modern architecture, said that 'form follows **function**'. The term 'functionalism' is used to describe the idea behind architecture which primarily focuses on the purpose of a building. However, many people disagree with this and feel that beauty is a more important factor in architectural design. In the modern world, it seems that most architects try to combine both ideas, aiming to create buildings which are both functional and **inspiring** in their beauty.

2 The reason for creating a building in the first place – its use – is clearly very important. When building an airport terminal, for example, you need to think of the needs of passengers as well as planes. Passengers want to get to their plane as quickly as they can, and planes need to be parked in a way which maximizes their ease of use. As such, many airport terminals have a circular shape with satellite areas. Residential homes need to have enough space for a family, art galleries need wall space to show pictures and factories need to produce goods as efficiently as possible. Each type of building has a different function, and, therefore, it has a different form.

3 On the other hand, many people believe that architects have a wider responsibility to society than just designing functional buildings. Beautiful, well-constructed buildings are a symbol of a **civilized** society and they **reflect** well **on** a business or the **reputation** of the owner. Ugly public buildings, however, can project a negative image of the organization. People say that living or working in an ugly place creates a **depressing** and uninspiring environment. In contrast, an attractive building can make people feel happier and increase their motivation to work.

4 In theory, there seems to be no reason why architecture cannot be both functional and beautiful. Yet in practice, this can cause problems. The Modern International style of the 1920s and 1930s, an example of which is the Guggenheim Museum in New York, was supposed to combine beauty with function. Many consider the museum's white spiral ramp beautiful, but there have been complaints that it is impractical, as it is difficult to stand back to view the art. Also, the ramp is so narrow that it can become overcrowded. The Farnsworth House by Ludwig Mies van der Rohe is another icon of beautiful design which **demonstrates** the idea that 'less is more'. However, critics have attacked it for a lack of privacy because of the huge glass windows. It also has a leaky flat roof and has been repeatedly flooded. It seems that even these two celebrated designs have problems with functionality.

5 If architects focus only on function, buildings may be cold, ugly and uninteresting. There is no doubt that a building with a beautiful form is something we can all appreciate. On the other hand, if they focus only on making it look beautiful, the building may be completely impractical. Therefore, blending these two ideas is necessary to create the perfect piece of architecture.

The Guggenheim Museum

The Farnsworth House

WHILE READING

SUMMARIZING

4 Read the essay again. Then complete the summary.

While some architecture values (1)__________ over form, there is an opposing view that the (2)__________ of a building is more important than its functionality. In practice, most (3)__________ strive for a combination of both ideas.

Architects feel that they are expected to design attractive buildings. The appearance of a building can (4)__________ either positively or negatively on its owner. Also, it can have an impact on the users' (5)__________ , which affects motivation.

Still, the first consideration in the design of a (6)__________ should be its purpose. The physical space should allow its (7)__________ to function as efficiently and comfortably as possible.

Although form *and* function is obviously the ideal, it is not always so easy to achieve, as shortcomings in several (8)__________ buildings have shown.

UNDERSTANDING PARAPHRASE

5 Match the original sentences (1–6) from the text to the correct paraphrases (a–f).

Original sentences

1 Beautiful, well-constructed buildings are a symbol of a civilized society.
2 People say that living or working in an ugly place creates a depressing and uninspiring environment.
3 Many people believe that architects have a wider responsibility to society than just designing functional buildings.
4 'Less is more'.
5 It seems that even these two celebrated designs have problems with functionality.
6 Each type of building has a different function, and, therefore, it has a different form.

Paraphrases

_____ a Unattractive buildings can make people feel unhappy and bored.
_____ b Attractive, safe buildings represent a cultured society.
_____ c A minimalist design can actually create a more powerful effect.
_____ d Every construction has a different purpose, and is therefore designed according to different criteria.
_____ e These famous buildings may have won awards, but they still do not always fulfil users' needs.
_____ f People who design buildings have a duty to the general public.

READING BETWEEN THE LINES

MAKING INFERENCES

6 Work with a partner. Answer the questions.

1 Why are well-designed buildings advantageous for the owner?

____

2 Why is a circular or 'satellite' shape beneficial for an airport terminal?

____

3 Why might governments demolish ugly public buildings?

____

4 What elements of a building could make it depressing?

____

5 Why could the design of a building increase your motivation to work?

____

DISCUSSION

SYNTHESIZING

7 Work with a partner. Use ideas from Reading 1 and Reading 2 to discuss the questions.

1 Would you want to live in the Farnsworth House? Why / Why not?
2 Do you agree that architects have a 'wider responsibility' to society, or should they just do what their clients want? Why?
3 Which is more important for you: a 'green' home which is eco-friendly, or one which is beautiful to look at? Why?

LANGUAGE DEVELOPMENT

ACADEMIC WORD FAMILIES

VOCABULARY

When you learn new words, you should also try to learn other words in the same word family. If you learn the noun *combination*, you should also try to learn the verb (*combine*) and the adjective (*combined*).

Architects aim for a **combination** of beauty and functionality. (noun)
Architects should **combine** beauty and functionality. (verb)
The **combined** beauty and functionality make this a perfect building. (adjective)

1 Complete the word families in the table.

noun	verb	adjective	adverb
function, functionalism	function	functional	functionally
environment		(1) ________	(2) ________
(3) ________	(4) ________	depressing	(5) ________
responsibility		(6) ________	(7) ________
architect, (8) ________		(9) ________	(10) ________
(11) ________		(12) ________	efficiently

PLUS

2 Complete the sentences with words from the table in Exercise 1.

1 It is important to consider the ________ impact of any new building on its natural surroundings.
2 ________ is an architectural system which believes that function is more important than beauty.
3 Environmentally friendly buildings usually use energy very ________ .
4 Architects need to plan buildings ________ in order to ensure that they are sustainable.
5 Badly designed buildings can ________ even the happiest person.
6 One famous critic described ________ as 'frozen music', meaning the design of a building is artistic.
7 Architects must consider the impact of buildings on the ________ .
8 Employers must be ________ for providing safe working areas.
9 Ugly and dark office designs may cause ________ in workers.
10 Certain details of ________ styles change all the time, but most key principles of architecture remain the same.

ARCHITECTURE AND PLANNING VOCABULARY

3 Work in pairs. Complete the definitions with the words from the box. Use the Glossary on pages 196–198 to help you.

amenities	green belt	outskirts	skyscrapers
structural engineer	suburban	urban sprawl	

1 A person whose job it is to help build an architect's design is a ____________ .
2 ____________ are very tall modern buildings in cities.
3 When cities spread out into the countryside, and car parks or new buildings replace forests and fields, the result is called ____________ .
4 A ____________ is a band of unspoilt countryside which may not be built on.
5 ____________ neighbourhoods are not located within a city. They are found on the ____________ of a city and usually have houses rather than apartment buildings.
6 Public ____________ are facilities that people enjoy living near, such as libraries, swimming pools and playgrounds.

4 Complete the sentences with your own ideas.

1 The key responsibility of an architect is ____________ .
2 When building skyscrapers, it is important to ____________ .
3 Conservation may be expensive, but ____________ .
4 Green belt land is important because ____________ .
5 Important amenities which should be provided by the government include ____________ .
6 Urban sprawl has a negative effect on the environment because ____________ .

PLUS

WRITING

CRITICAL THINKING

At the end of this unit, you will write a persuasive essay. Look at this unit's writing task below.

Which is more important when building or buying a new home: its location or its size?

SKILLS

Creating a persuasive argument

To make the argument of your essay as persuasive as possible, focus on your most convincing points, and make sure they are supported with reliable and relevant evidence.

ANALYZE

1 Look at Reading 2 again. Using the information there, plus your own ideas, write down in the T-chart the advantages of focusing on either the beauty or the function of a building.

Advantages of focusing on beauty	Advantages of focusing on function
Beautiful buildings can put us in a good mood.	

EVALUATE

2 In each column, which idea is the most persuasive? Which idea is the least persuasive?

ANALYZE

3 Now look at the Writing task. With a partner, discuss the advantages of focusing on location and the advantages of focusing on size when planning a new building. Write notes in the T-chart below.

Advantages of focusing on location	Advantages of focusing on size

4 Highlight the ideas in your T-chart that you think are the most persuasive. Write an *X* next to the ideas you think are the least persuasive.

EVALUATE

GRAMMAR FOR WRITING

REGISTER IN ACADEMIC WRITING

GRAMMAR

The types of language used in informal writing and formal, academic written English are very different. Informal writing tends to be similar to speaking, whereas in formal written English, writers usually use the following:

- longer, more complex sentences
- more precise, technical words
- more formal phrases and linking words

Meanwhile writers usually avoid the following:

- slang and colloquial expressions such as *cool*, *awesome* or *stuff*
- phrasal verbs (unless there is no alternative word)
- first-person personal pronouns (*I* and *me*)
- contractions such as *they're* instead of *they are*, or *it's* instead of *it is*
- the terms *a lot of* or *lots of*
- exclamation marks (*!*)
- the terms *et cetera* or *etc.*

1 Read the text below. Match the informal words and phrases in bold (1–11) with the correct academic words and phrases in the box.

approximately _____ calculate _____ can be justified _____
considerable investment _____ critical _____
and desire to work effectively _____ fundamentally _____
has a positive impact on _____ there is no real benefit _____
this supports the accuracy of this notion _____ undoubtedly _____

Choosing an architect is (1) **basically** about cost for many organizations. (2) **I'm sure that** the initial cost is (3) **really important,** regardless of whether the building is for the private or public sector. Good architecture requires (4) **lots of money**, and institutions have to (5) **work out** whether high costs (6) **are worth it** in the long term. Some people claim that (7) **there's not much point** in providing an attractive working area. However, others would argue that a pleasant working environment (8) **is good for** people's moods and, therefore, their productivity, (9) **etc.** A recent survey in a multinational IT company suggested that (10) **around** 75% of employees took this view. (11) **That's a lot of people!**

2 Complete the sentences with your own ideas.

1 Fundamentally, good buildings are those that ______________________ .
2 It is difficult to calculate ______________________ .
3 One thing which is critical when designing new buildings is ______________________ .
4 The installation costs of solar panels can only be justified if ______________________ .
5 Architecture can have a positive impact on ______________________ .
6 There is no real benefit in ______________________ .

ACADEMIC WRITING SKILLS

ORDERING INFORMATION

SKILLS

To make writing fluent, academic writers often refer back to the previous sentence when it has the same topic. Look at the examples:

When choosing a new house, the most important consideration may be location. **Areas near good schools** are often popular.
For many people the first criterion is **size**. **The number of bedrooms** may be determined by family size.

The beginning of the second sentence is a paraphrase of the end of the first one. Sometimes writers just use a reference word such as *this*, *that*, *these*, *those* or reference phrases like *That is why*, *For this reason* or *In spite of this*.

Some families prefer to expand their existing houses. **This** allows all family members to live together.
Living in a large city can mean parking problems. **In spite of this**, many people are drawn to urban areas.

PLUS

1 Write the phrases in the best places in the text.

for this reason	in spite of this	it	this combination	this profession

Architecture is often said to be a difficult subject to study. (1)______________________ , many people choose to go into (2)______________________ . While some subjects are more quantitative, such as Engineering, and others are more creative, such as Art, Architecture involves both. (3)______________________ may be what attracts people to (4)______________________ as a career. Architects are in charge of creating the designs of all of the buildings we see every day. (5)______________________ , they play an important role in our communities.

2 Circle the best option out of the two choices in the paragraph.

The classical architecture of Ancient Greece remains influential for architects today. (1) *This style / This event* was based on a system made up of columns. Although (2) *the columns / the Greeks* may seem simple, ancient architects made them beautiful by carving them with mythological creatures and other images. (3) *They / It* created some of the most detailed designs in the history of architecture. The interest that (4) *these Greek architects / these columns* had in simplicity and proportion in their buildings was later very influential for architects in Ancient Rome. The Romans gave five names to their architectural styles: Doric, Ionic, Corinthian, Tuscan and Composite. Roman-style columns, domes and arches have since been part of the designs of important, more modern buildings across the world. In Paris, for example, the Arc de Triomphe and the Place Vendôme are examples of Roman-looking architecture. (5) *These structures / These Romans* were built during the reign of Emperor Napoleon to make Paris look like the 'New Rome'.

PRIORITIZING ARGUMENTS

SKILLS

Writers need to think about how to support a point of view by following it with specific facts or observations which can persuade the reader.

For example, this statement expressing a writer's point of view needs support in order to be persuasive:

It is important for us to continue to construct environmentally friendly buildings.

If the writer follows his or her point of view with the sentence below, it would not be very persuasive:

This is because they are good.

However, if the writer follows his or her point of view with the sentence below, it would be much more persuasive:

This is because they help reduce carbon emissions, cause less harm to our environment and use fewer irreplaceable fossil fuels.

By saying that he or she thinks that something is good, the writer is just confirming his or her opinion. This is not especially persuasive. In contrast, offering facts as support for the argument appeals to the reader's sense of logic. This is a more persuasive technique.

3 Read the sentences in bold. Then decide which follow-up sentence sounds more persuasive.

1 **Small homes can be crowded.**
   a This lack of space can cause family tensions.
   b We should live in large houses, so everybody has plenty of space.
2 **Homes should be near shops and schools.**
   a Fuel use can be decreased and costs can be saved if we do not have to drive.
   b Being able to access these amenities without a car is a bonus.
3 **It is better to live in spacious buildings**.
   a Large open rooms allow families to spend more time together, which enhances family unity.
   b People can spend more time together if they have large open rooms.
4 **An apartment without windows is undesirable.**
   a This is because you cannot look outside; you can only look at walls.
   b If you can see outside, you can see the weather, which sometimes lifts your mood.
5 **Ideally, we need homes which are convenient for travelling to work.**
   a Accessibility is an important everyday need, and it will save us valuable time.
   b We often cannot choose to live near our workplace.

4 Which side of an argument would each sentence persuade the reader to agree with? Circle *a*, *b* or *c*.

a = The environment is more important.
b = Minimizing cost is more important.
c = Both are equally important.

1 The construction company has to make a profit, so it should construct buildings cheaply. a b c
2 Eco-buildings may encourage people to be more environmentally responsible in their day-to-day lives. a b c
3 Environmentally friendly buildings cost less in the long run due to energy savings. a b c
4 Because of the global population increase, we urgently need more buildings; if they are expensive, they may not be built. a b c
5 Cheaply constructed buildings have a shorter lifespan and may need to be destroyed sooner. a b c
6 The government may provide financial support for eco-building projects. a b c

WRITING TASK

Which is more important when building or buying a new home: its location or its size?

PLAN

1 Look back at your notes in Critical thinking. Create an outline for your essay using the structure below. In paragraphs 2 and 3, put your arguments in order of how persuasive you think they are.

Paragraph 1: Introduction

Paragraph 2: Arguments in favour of location being more important.

____

____

____

____

____

____

Paragraph 3: Arguments in favour of size being more important.

____

____

____

____

____

____

Paragraph 4: Your position and conclusions.

____

____

____

____

____

____

2 Refer to the Task checklist on page 122 as you prepare your essay.

WRITE A FIRST DRAFT

3 Write your essay. Write 350–400 words.

REVISE

4 Use the Task checklist to review your essay for content and structure.

TASK CHECKLIST	✔
Does your essay follow the structure provided?	
Do your arguments reflect both sides of the question?	
Did you order information correctly?	
Did you prioritize your arguments in order of how persuasive you think they are?	
Do your examples adequately support your ideas?	

5 Make any necessary changes to your essay.

EDIT

6 Use the Language checklist to edit your essay for language errors.

LANGUAGE CHECKLIST	✔
Did you spell different words from the same word family correctly?	
Did you use subject-specific language correctly?	
Did you use formal academic language?	
Do references to subjects in previous sentences use pronouns correctly?	

7 Make any necessary changes to your essay.

OBJECTIVES REVIEW

8 Check your learning objectives for this unit. Write *3*, *2* or *1* for each objective.

3 = very well 2 = well 1 = not so well

I can …

watch and understand a video about government grants for energy-efficient homes.	____
skim a text.	____
create a persuasive argument.	____
use correct register in academic writing.	____
order information.	____
prioritize arguments.	____
write a persuasive essay.	____

9 Use the *Unlock* Digital Workbook for more practice with this unit's learning objectives.

UNLOCK ONLINE

WORDLIST

amenities (n)	depression (n) ⊙	relevant (adj) ⊙
architectural (adj) ⊙	durable (adj)	reputation (n) ⊙
architecturally (adv)	efficiency (n) ⊙	responsibility (n) ⊙
architecture (n) ⊙	efficient (adj) ⊙	responsible (adj) ⊙
civilized (adj)	environmental (adj) ⊙	second-hand (adj)
compromise (n) ⊙	environmentally (adv)	sector (n) ⊙
conservation (n) ⊙	function (n) ⊙	skyscrapers (n)
demonstrate (v) ⊙	green belt (n phr)	structural engineer (n phr)
depress (v)	inspiring (adj)	suburban (adj)
depressing (adj)	outskirts (n)	urban sprawl (n phr)
depressingly (adv)	reflect on (phr v)	

⊙ = high-frequency words in the Cambridge Academic Corpus

LEARNING OBJECTIVES	IN THIS UNIT YOU WILL ...
Watch and listen	watch and understand a video about wind power.
Reading skill	work out meaning from context.
Critical thinking	evaluate benefits and drawbacks; organize ideas for an essay.
Grammar	use defining and non-defining relative clauses.
Academic writing skills	introduce advantages and disadvantages; make academic writing coherent.
Writing task	write an advantages and disadvantages essay.

ENERGY

UNIT 6

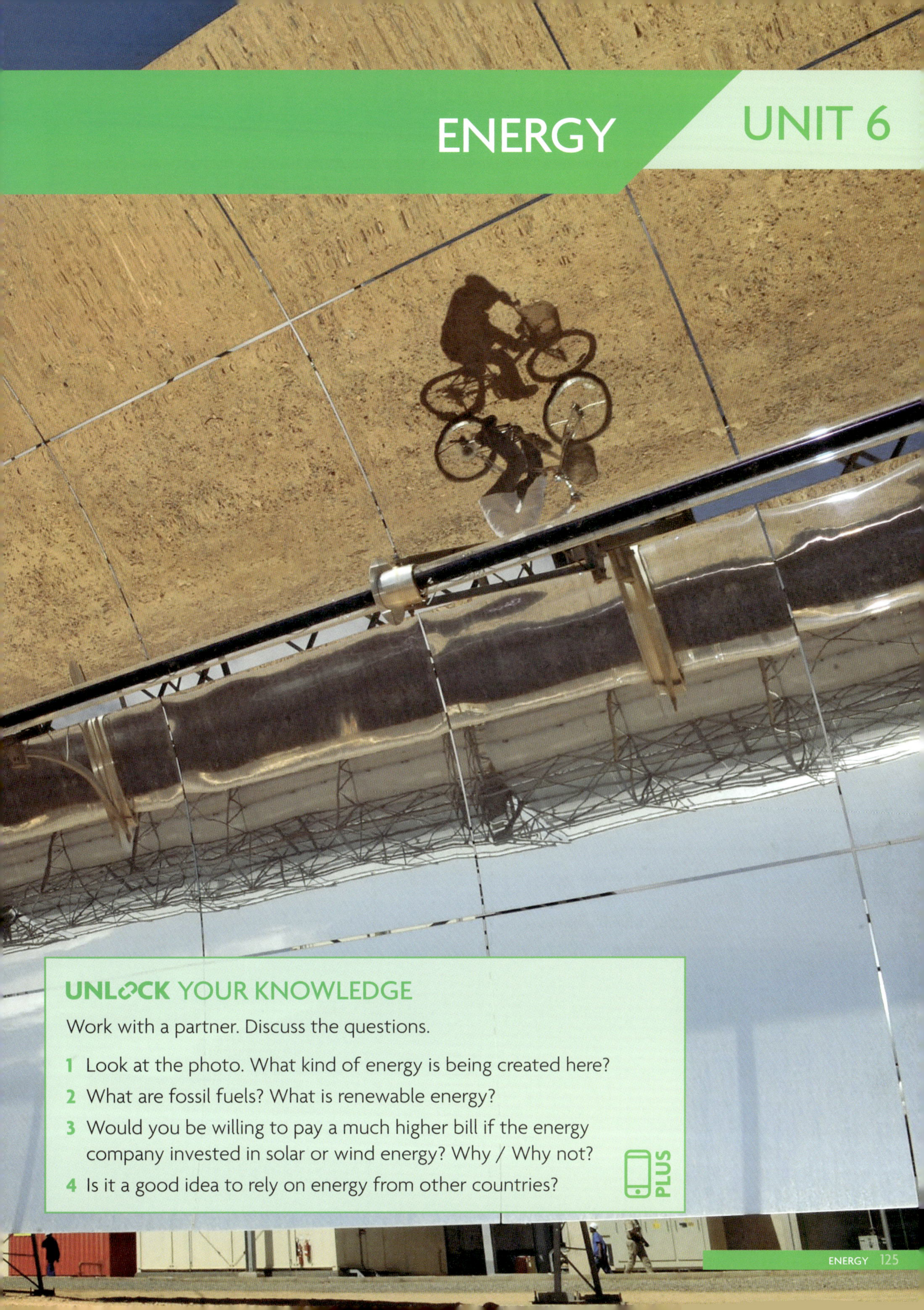

UNLOCK YOUR KNOWLEDGE

Work with a partner. Discuss the questions.

1 Look at the photo. What kind of energy is being created here?
2 What are fossil fuels? What is renewable energy?
3 Would you be willing to pay a much higher bill if the energy company invested in solar or wind energy? Why / Why not?
4 Is it a good idea to rely on energy from other countries?

PLUS

WATCH AND LISTEN

PREPARING TO WATCH

ACTIVATING YOUR KNOWLEDGE

1 Circle the statements that you agree with. Discuss your answers with a partner.

1 Our society uses more energy than it did ten years ago.
2 We have more devices that use electricity than we did ten years ago.
3 There are many alternatives to fossil fuels.
4 Fossil fuels are the cheapest source of energy.
5 It is not a problem to depend on one main energy source.
6 Wind and solar power will be our main sources of energy in the future.

PREDICTING CONTENT USING VISUALS

2 Look at the pictures from the video. Discuss the questions with a partner.

1 What is the difference between the first and third pictures?
2 What does the second picture show?
3 Who do you think the person in the final picture is? What do you think she is talking about?

GLOSSARY

renewable energy (n) energy that is produced using the sun, wind, etc., or from crops, rather than using fossil fuels such as oil or coal

overtake (v) to go past something by being larger or faster

smart technology (phr) smart technology uses computers and information in electronic form

continue unabated (v) to keep going without becoming weaker or less

WHILE WATCHING

UNDERSTANDING MAIN IDEAS

3 Watch the video. Write *T* (true) or *F* (false) or *DNS* (does not say) next to the statements below. Correct the false statements.

_____ 1 Wind power provides almost 10% of the world's energy.
_____ 2 The UK gets more electricity from wind than from coal.
_____ 3 The UK's emission rates are decreasing.
_____ 4 Wind power is less expensive than traditional sources of energy.
_____ 5 Wind power presents some risks to health and safety.
_____ 6 The UK is a leader in offshore wind power.

UNDERSTANDING DETAIL

4 Watch again. Write a supporting detail for each main idea.

1 Wind power is a good alternative to fossil fuels.
____
2 The UK is an especially good place to develop wind power.
____
3 In some ways, offshore wind power is preferable to onshore wind power.
____
4 Wind power does have some disadvantages.
____

MAKING INFERENCES

5 Work with a partner. Discuss the questions. Give reasons for your answers.

1 Why do you think there is widespread public support for this form of energy? Why is there also opposition?
2 The energy analyst in the video claims that 'you won't find an energy analyst out there that disagrees' with a vision of the future that depends on renewables. Why can she make this statement with such confidence?

DISCUSSION

6 Work with a partner and answer the questions. Give reasons for your answers.

1 Do you think a wind turbine near your home would be a good idea? Why / Why not?
2 Are there some places in the world that could benefit from wind power more than others?
3 Should communities have a choice about whether wind turbines are installed near them?
4 Do you think the use of wind power is likely to increase in the future?

READING

READING 1

PREPARING TO READ

PREDICTING CONTENT USING VISUALS

1 You are going to read an article on renewable energy. Look at the photos. Match the types of renewable energy in the box to the correct photo.

geothermal energy	hydropower	solar power	wind power

1 ______________

2 ______________

3 ______________

4 ______________

UNDERSTANDING KEY VOCABULARY

2 Read the sentences and write the words in bold next to the definitions.

1 **Aquatic** creatures include fish, dolphins and whales.
2 Oil companies often drill **offshore** to get petroleum from the sea floor.
3 Energy from the sun is considered an **inexhaustible** resource; as long as the sun is there, it can give us energy.
4 The **initial** response to the recycling programme has been good. Now let's see what happens next.
5 Waterfalls **generate** energy which we can use as power.
6 All countries around the world need energy sources for their cars, machines and appliances. This need is **universal**.
7 Many people think that we need to **utilize** existing renewable energy sources such as solar and wind power.

a ______________ (adj) at the beginning; first
b ______________ (v) to cause to exist; produce
c ______________ (adj) living in, happening in or connected with water
d ______________ (adv) away from or at a distance from the land
e ______________ (adj) existing everywhere or involving everyone
f ______________ (v) to make use of something
g ______________ (adj) in such large amounts that it cannot be used up

HYDROPOWER

1 Hydropower is created when moving water turns turbines to create electricity. The source of the moving water can be rivers, waterfalls or the sea. Because flowing water continues to move, this creates an **inexhaustible** amount of energy which can be stored and used when the demand is highest. There are a few drawbacks, however. Water-powered turbines can have a negative environmental impact on **aquatic** wildlife and can endanger boats. Also, creating hydropower dams causes land behind the dams to permanently flood. Finally, it is expensive to set up hydropower systems – the average cost is between $1 million and $4 million.

WIND POWER

2 To create wind power, large turbines are placed on top of hills or **offshore**. The wind turns the blades, which **generate** energy. Wind turbines can be **utilized** on a large scale or on a small scale. Unlike hydropower, this process is relatively cheap and is considered one of the most affordable forms of electricity today. Also, it does not harm the air or land it uses. However, many people consider wind turbines ugly and noisy. Also, they rely on the wind, so if it is not windy, no energy is produced. Finally, like hydropower, wind turbines can be a threat to wildlife such as local birds.

SOLAR ENERGY

3 To use solar energy, solar panels absorb sunlight and, using devices called *photovoltaic cells*, turn it into electricity. The sun produces energy constantly, which makes solar energy an inexhaustible resource. Another benefit is that it generates no pollution. Solar energy can be adapted to work on a variety of buildings and in a variety of environments. However, a large area of land is needed to produce a large amount of solar power. Scientists have determined that if we wanted to try to power the entire Earth with renewable solar power, we would need to cover a land area about the size of Spain with solar panels. In places with less sunlight, solar power generation has limitations. Also, photovoltaic cells are fragile and can be easily damaged.

BIOMASS ENERGY

4 Biomass is a biologically produced fuel made from plant and animal material, which is mostly composed of carbon, hydrogen and oxygen. It is the oldest source of renewable energy, used since humans first started burning wood for fire. Today, steam from burning biomass – made up of rubbish and other organic waste, rather than wood – turns turbines, generating electricity. Biomass can re-grow over a relatively short period of time compared to the hundreds of millions of years that it takes for fossil fuels to form. It is also an efficient way to generate power, and it is **universal**. Another benefit is that it reduces the need to bury rubbish under the ground in a landfill. However, some people are concerned that burning biomass contributes to global warming because it produces greenhouse gases[1]. Also, using biomass to generate energy on a large scale can be expensive.

GEOTHERMAL ENERGY

5 With geothermal energy, heat which is trapped in the ground can be converted into steam to turn turbines. The power it generates can then be used to produce electricity and heat buildings. Geothermal energy uses relatively simple technology. Like several of the other energy sources already mentioned, this process causes no pollution and is inexhaustible. The most active geothermal resources are usually found in areas near volcanoes or where geothermal activity naturally occurs. The largest area of this kind is known as the 'Ring of Fire'. It rims the Pacific Ocean and is bounded by eastern Asia and the western edge of the Americas. Outside of regions like these, geothermal energy is usually unavailable. The **initial** costs of installing a geothermal energy system are very high, but once it is built, the running costs are low.

GEOTHERMAL REGIONS OF THE WORLD

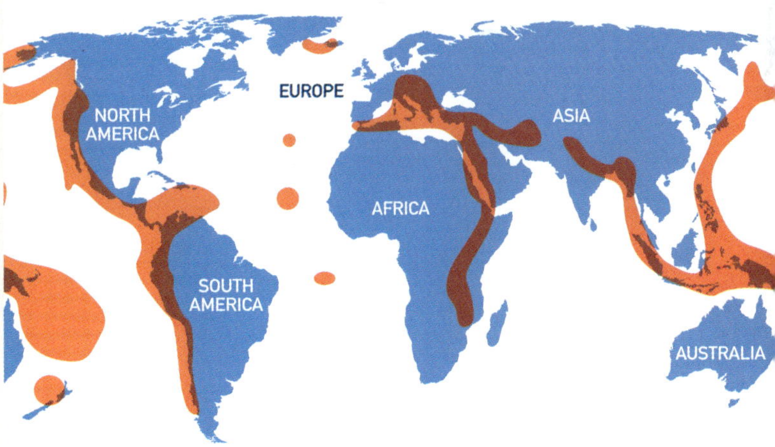

[1]**greenhouse gases** (n) gases, such as carbon dioxide, which cause a gradual warming of the Earth's atmosphere

WHILE READING

READING FOR MAIN IDEAS

3 Read the article and choose the best title.

a 'Why are fossil fuels running out?'
b 'The disadvantages of clean energy generation'
c 'An overview of renewable energy production'
d 'The benefits of renewable energy sources'
e 'The pros and cons of environmental conservation'

READING FOR DETAIL

4 Read the article again. Which types of renewable energy do the sentences describe? Write the correct type next to each sentence.

1 This source of energy can be used for many purposes and will last forever, but it cannot work 24 hours a day. ___________
2 This type of energy produces greenhouse gases, but disposes of waste. ___________
3 This type of energy which is based on steam-powered turbines is expensive to set up but cheap to operate. ___________
4 This type of energy may require some people to relocate. ___________
5 This type of energy may be more common or relevant in countries which have deserts or are near the equator. ___________
6 This type of energy is expensive to begin with, although the technology is relatively basic. ___________

5 Match each newspaper headline to a renewable energy source. Write the correct type of energy next to each headline.

1 'Wave-power machines struggle in marine environment' ___________
2 'Rare eagle struck by newly constructed turbine' ___________
3 'Report shows 10,000 kg of waste used last year to fuel energy plant' ___________
4 'Amazing summer weather creates a huge supply of energy' ___________
5 'Government pledges millions for new plant near volcano' ___________
6 'Low rainfall suggests high electricity prices' ___________
7 'Environmentalists question the ability of this bio-energy source to renew itself' ___________

READING BETWEEN THE LINES

SKILLS

Working out meaning from context

When you read a word you do not understand, you could look in a dictionary, but this will slow down your reading, and cause you to lose your place. Instead, try to guess the meaning from the context. Often you do not need the exact meaning of the word to be able to understand the sentence.

- Look at the surrounding words for meaning clues.
  *It is also an efficient way to **generate** power, and it is universal.*
- Try to substitute a word so that the sentence still makes sense.
  *The wind turns the blades, which **generate** (create) energy.*
- Look for a comparison or contrast between two sentence halves.
  *Water-powered turbines can have a negative environmental impact on aquatic wildlife and can **endanger** boats.*
- Use linking words or conjunctions to help you guess the meaning.
  *Although the government has **pledged** to build a new wind farm, some believe this will not happen.*

WORKING OUT MEANING

6 Read the article again and find the following words. See if you can identify their meaning, and highlight any other words in the text which helped you guess the meaning.

1 solar ______
2 fragile ______
3 stored ______
4 geothermal ______
5 wildlife ______
6 bury ______
7 bounded by ______

DISCUSSION

7 Work with a partner. Discuss the questions.

1 Which types of renewable energy would be the most appropriate alternative to fossil fuels in your area?
2 How will the growing global population affect the type of energy sources which can be used?
3 What is more important when considering energy use: cost or impact on the environment? Why?

PLUS

READING 2

PREPARING TO READ

UNDERSTANDING KEY VOCABULARY

1 Read the definitions. Complete the sentences with the correct form of the words in bold.

> **address** (v) to give attention to or to deal with a matter or problem
> **adopt** (v) to accept or begin to use something
> **alarming** (adj) causing worry or fear
> **diminish** (v) to reduce or be reduced in size or importance
> **instigate** (v) to cause an event or situation to happen
> **resistant** (adj) not accepting of something
> **urgent** (adj) needing immediate attention
> **vital** (adj) necessary or extremely important for the success or continued existence of something

1 Environmentalists feel that finding solutions to fight climate change is a(n) __________ issue and needs to be addressed right now.
2 Many people find global warming __________ because the future of planet Earth could be in danger.
3 The government plans to __________ a recycling programme similar to the one Germany has and is also looking into building wind turbines.
4 Over one hundred United Nations delegates signed a document to __________ climate change and establish new environmental standards.
5 The aim of this plan is to __________ pollution to lower levels.
6 Many people say it is __________ for the survival of certain plant and animal species that we stop pollution caused by factories.
7 Manufacturers may be __________ to using more 'green' production methods, so we need new laws which force them to do it.
8 The 1962 book *Silent Spring* by Rachel Carson __________ the modern environmental movement.

PLUS

USING YOUR KNOWLEDGE

2 What do you think will happen when the world starts to run out of these resources?

1 oil *prices will rise; petrol will be more expensive*
2 water __________
3 trees __________
4 food __________
5 metal __________

3 Work in a small group. Think about how the lack of the following resources can cause shortages in some places. How can people address these different problems? When you have finished, share your ideas with the rest of the class.

1 oil *invest in renewable resources like wind energy*
2 water ______
3 trees ______
4 food ______
5 metal ______

4 Work in pairs. You are going to read an essay which discusses the Reduce, Reuse, Recycle strategy. Discuss what you think this means. Think of examples of things you can reduce, reuse or recycle.

5 Read the essay on page 134 and check your answers.

WHILE READING

READING FOR MAIN IDEAS

6 Work with a partner. Answer the questions.

1 Does the writer think that one of the methods (reducing, reusing or recycling) is better than the others?
2 What are some drawbacks offered for relying on alternative energy sources?
3 What is the writer's final conclusion on this topic?

READING FOR DETAIL

7 Complete the student's notes about the article.

1 INTRO: To better manage the world's resources, we need to 'reduce, *reuse* , recycle'.
2 PARA. 2: Use fewer resources – save electricity, use less water, avoid ______ transport.
3 PARA 3: Reuse items, e.g., glass bottles – but be careful when reusing ______ equipment and ______ items.
4 PARA 4: Recycling paper and plastic is easy. Recycling rare ______ is harder and more dangerous.
5 PARA 5: We need to use more alternative and sustainable energy sources and fewer ______ .
6 PARA 6: Examples: hydropower, wind turbines, ______ energy, biomass, ______ energy
7 CONC: It is crucial to 'go green' for the future of ______ .

MAINTAINING OUR VITAL NATURAL RESOURCES

1 The world's natural resources are being used at an **alarming** rate – not only fossil fuels such as coal, oil and gas, but also water, wood, metals and minerals. This has many potential consequences for the billions of people who live on Earth. In recent years, both individuals and governments have become more interested in better managing the world's resources. While alternative energy solutions are important, they are not always feasible[1]. An immediate way to improve the situation is to encourage everyone to 'reduce, reuse, recycle'.

Reduce, reuse, recycle

2 We must all learn to use fewer natural resources on a day-to-day basis. We can start by reducing the number of electrical items we leave plugged in, using less water and avoiding motorized transport. Many cities are **instigating** carbon emissions taxes, which is a step in the right direction. In our homes, we can use only energy-saving light bulbs and install water meters. Parents need to train children from an early age to turn off lights which they are not using. It is sometimes difficult to persuade people to use less energy and water, or to eat less food, but an effective way to motivate people to **adopt** less wasteful practices is to make these essential commodities much more expensive.

3 It is often possible to restore old, unwanted objects to a state in which they can be used again. Glass bottles can be cleaned and reused without having to be broken and remade. Reusing things is a very efficient process and consumes less energy than recycling. It does, however, often require a lot of expensive organization and administration. There are also concerns to **address** regarding reused medical equipment and food-storage items, for example, because of safety and hygiene issues. Still, the benefits of reusing items are clear.

4 Most of us know that materials such as paper and plastic can be recycled into new products. This process uses less energy and emits fewer greenhouse gases than producing articles from raw materials. Yes, sorting through used materials before recycling them is a dirty and difficult job, and breaking up electronic equipment to recycle rare metals is time-consuming and potentially dangerous. But provided we understand the dangers involved, the necessity of recycling on a community scale is evident.

Alternative energy

5 A lot of attention has been paid in recent years to the dangers of relying on fossil fuels. For this reason, the use of alternatives to coal, oil and gas are becoming more and more common. Alternative energy sources can be recovered or produced without emitting carbon dioxide and contributing to global warming. They can decrease air pollution, which is better for our health, as it **diminishes** instances of asthma[2]. They are often sustainable resources as well, which means they will not get used up.

6 There are many examples of alternative energy sources. Hydropower utilizes the power of moving water such as waterfalls and rivers. Large turbines can be used to generate wind power. Solar energy uses panels which absorb sunlight and turn it into electricity by way of photovoltaic cells. The burning of biomass can be used to create steam. Finally, geothermal energy uses the heat within the earth to produce electricity and heat buildings. A particular type of alternative energy may work the best for a particular region. The other side of this is that some of these energy sources may not be available at all to people in certain places because of environmental limitations.

Let's not wait

7 To avoid a catastrophic[3] depletion of **vital** natural resources in the future, **urgent** action is required now. Alternative energy production is certainly essential, but it can be expensive and time-consuming to install the required elements. Some developing areas of the world may simply be unable to pay for it. In other places, corporations and taxpayers may be **resistant** to it. The 'reduce, reuse, recycle' strategy, at least for the present, seems to be a manageable one which can be practised by both individuals and organizations. People may be resistant to the idea of changing their ways or increasing the cost of their routines by 'going green', but it is crucial that we do this for the future of the planet.

[1]**feasible** (adj) possible, reasonable or likely
[2]**asthma** (n) an illness which makes it difficult to breathe
[3]**catastrophic** (adj) related to a sudden event which causes great suffering or destruction

READING BETWEEN THE LINES

MAKING INFERENCES

8 Work with a partner. Answer the questions based on ideas in the essay.

1 Why will energy need to become more expensive before people are motivated to reduce the energy they use?
2 Why should we avoid the use of motorized transport?
3 Why might it be dangerous to reuse medical equipment?
4 Why might corporations which manufacture products be resistant to environmental laws?

DISCUSSION

SYNTHESIZING

9 Work with a partner. Use ideas from Reading 1 and Reading 2 to discuss the questions.

1 Is recycling common in your country? Do you recycle? What objects can be recycled?
2 Do you think it is fair to penalize people financially if they do not recycle? Can you think of any other objects that can be reused without having to recycle them?
3 When thinking about energy, what considerations are more important: the appearance and design of the source, or the environmental impact? Why?

LANGUAGE DEVELOPMENT

ENERGY COLLOCATIONS

1 Match the nouns in the box to the correct group (1–6) of words.

energy	fuel	pollution	problem	production	source

1 fossil / diesel / alternative / renewable / clean ________
2 renewable / green / nuclear / solar / geothermal ________
3 environmental / air / industrial / water / radioactive ________
4 energy / fuel / power / water / renewable ________
5 electricity / energy / oil / gas / agricultural ________
6 serious / health / environmental / major / medical ________

2 Complete the sentences using energy collocations from Exercise 1.

1 Critics of __________ energy say that the risks to the environment outweigh the benefits of cheap electricity.
2 Asthma and diabetes are increasingly common __________ problems.
3 For a renewable __________ of electricity to be truly successful, governments have to invest more money in it.
4 __________ fuels, such as oil and gas, have a finite lifespan.
5 __________ energy, whichever renewable source it comes from, tends to be slightly more expensive for the user.
6 Rivers and lakes are two major __________ sources which can be used for hydroelectric power.

PLUS

FORMAL AND INFORMAL ACADEMIC VERBS

3 Match formal verbs (1–8) with informal alternatives (a–h).

1 consult	a get
2 contest	b skip; leave out
3 deliver	c start
4 diminish	d look at
5 instigate	e use
6 omit	f decrease
7 secure	g give
8 utilize	h disagree with

4 Complete the sentences with the correct forms of the formal verbs in Exercise 3.

1 Resources are beginning to __________ ; soon they will run out.
2 This company needs to __________ its energy policy to the government by the end of the year.
3 The application to construct a wind farm in this area has been __________ by local residents who dislike the idea.
4 If people __________ the documents on our website, they can see how biofuel is made.
5 The rise in fuel prices should __________ a debate on oil reserves.
6 This car __________ fuel more efficiently than previous models.
7 Advocates of biofuels sometimes __________ key details such as how much land is needed to cultivate the crops. People who disagree with them would certainly use this information to argue against biofuel advocates.
8 This country must __________ new renewable energy sources.

PLUS

WRITING

CRITICAL THINKING

At the end of this unit, you will write an explanatory essay. Look at this unit's writing task below.

Explain the advantages and disadvantages of three types of renewable energy and decide which would work best in your country.

1 Read the questions in the table. Look back at Reading 1 and Reading 2 to help you complete the table. Give reasons for your ideas.

ANALYZE

	What are the benefits?	What are the drawbacks?	Is it effective for your country? What is the impact of producing it?
hydropower			
wind power			
solar energy			
biomass energy			
geothermal energy			

2 Compare your answers with a partner. Do his or her answers provide you with any extra information? If so, add this information to your table.

SKILLS

Evaluating benefits and drawbacks

When planning certain kinds of essays, you may be required to analyze specific benefits and drawbacks. Doing this can help you identify whether something is generally positive or negative, and for what reason. Collect the points you wish to make and organize them. Then, put them in order of importance, usefulness or interest.

3 Review your notes and decide on the three best options for your country from the energy sources below. Compare your answers with a partner.

EVALUATE

- hydropower
- wind
- solar
- biomass
- geothermal

ANALYZE

4 Focus on your top three sources of energy. Write a sentence for each one that says why you think it would be a suitable alternative energy choice for your country. Use ideas from Readings 1 and 2 to help you.

rank	type of energy	reason
1		
2		
3		

GRAMMAR FOR WRITING

RELATIVE CLAUSES

GRAMMAR

Relative clauses can define, describe or add extra information about nouns. In the sentence below, the part in bold is a relative clause.

Energy sources **which produce greenhouse gases** should not be used.

The relative clause (*which produce greenhouse gases*) gives important information about the subject (*energy sources*). Note that a relative clause must contain a subject and a verb, but it cannot be a sentence by itself.

Most relative clauses start with a relative pronoun (*who*, *which*, *that*, *whose*) or a relative adverb (*when*, *where*).

Use *who* or *that* for people.
Rachel Carson was the environmentalist **who/that wrote the book *Silent Spring***.

Use *which* or *that* for things or ideas.
This was the book **which/that instigated the modern environmental movement**.

Use *where* for places.
The UK is the country **where the first clean air law was passed**.

Use *when* for time.
The 1960s was the decade **when most people started paying attention to environmental issues for the first time**.

Use *whose* for possession.
A manufacturing company **whose factories pollute the environment** will have to pay penalties.

1 Underline the relative clause in each sentence and choose the correct relative pronoun. What subject does each relative clause refer to?

1 Enrico Fermi was the scientist *who* / *which* first split the atom.
2 The people *whose* / *where* houses are near nuclear power stations understandably worry about radioactive leaks.
3 The cabinet *which* / *where* the electricity meter is located is locked.
4 It is sometimes cheaper to use electricity at night *which* / *when* fewer people are using it.
5 Ethanol is a type of biofuel *which* / *who* is made from sugar found in certain crops.

GRAMMAR

There are two kinds of relative clauses: *defining* and *non-defining*.

Defining relative clauses

Defining relative clauses give essential information about a noun.

Wind turbines **which are offshore** are dangerous to marine mammals.

The defining relative clause here makes it clear which subject we are talking about (the offshore wind turbines, not the ones on land). If the clause is removed from the sentence, it would suggest that all wind turbines are dangerous to marine mammals, even the ones on land. So, the relative clause defines or identifies *which* wind turbines we mean.

Non-defining relative clauses

Non-defining relative clauses provide extra, non-essential information about a noun.

Wind turbines, **which may be offshore**, provide clean, renewable energy.

In this sentence, the most important information is that wind turbines provide clean, renewable energy. The information in the relative clause is non-essential. It provides extra information about wind turbines (i.e. they may be offshore). If the clause is removed, the rest of the sentence still makes sense. Use commas before and after non-defining relative clauses.

Do not use *that* in non-defining relative clauses. Use *who* for people and *which* for things.

Rachel Carson, **who wrote *Silent Spring***, began her career as a biologist.

Nuclear energy, **which is primarily generated by splitting atoms**, provides 11% of the world's energy supplies.

✗ Nuclear energy, ~~**that**~~ **which** **is primarily generated by splitting atoms**, provides 11% of the world's energy supplies.

2 Complete the sentences with the correct relative pronoun. Then add commas to the sentences which contain non-defining relative clauses.

1 Nuclear power stations __________ have poor safety records should be closed down.
2 Solar power __________ is a form of renewable energy is very popular in southern Spain.
3 There are certain solar panels __________ can produce almost a kilowatt of electricity per day.
4 Wind turbines __________ are located offshore are more expensive than wind turbines which are located on top of hills.
5 People __________ criticize nuclear power should consult the facts.
6 Al Gore __________ is a key supporter of alternative energy won the Nobel Prize in 2007.

3 Read the text below and circle the correct relative pronouns.

Lately, the government of China has been emphasizing the importance of using more renewable power, (1) *which / that* it defines as the mix of hydro, nuclear, wind and solar power. Mr Lin Boqiang, (2) *which / who* represents the Centre of China Energy Economics Research at Xiamen University, has pointed out that the country, (3) *which / that* is the most populous in the world, hopes to reach 80% renewable power by 2050. In order to reach this goal, the country will need to increase its use of the power sources (4) *where / that* it uses the least. These are wind and solar, (5) *which / who* are currently only a small component of the electricity mix. At present, China still generates more than 70% of its electricity from coal, (6) *which / that* is a fossil fuel.

ACADEMIC WRITING SKILLS

INTRODUCING ADVANTAGES AND DISADVANTAGES

SKILLS

You can use a range of phrases to introduce the advantages and disadvantages of ideas or solutions to problems.

One **major** advantage of ... is ...
The **most obvious** benefits of ... are ...
One **other apparent** advantage of ... is ...
A **further possible** benefit of ... is ...
The **most serious** disadvantage of ... is ...
A **distinct** drawback of ... is ...
One **other inherent** disadvantage of ... is ...
Another **potential** drawback of ... is ...

Notice how adjectives like *apparent*, *possible* and *potential* can be used to show less certain or less obvious advantages and disadvantages.

1 Use the prompts to create sentences. Use the phrases from the skills box opposite to help you.

1 advantage / wind power / inexhaustible / never run out
One advantage of wind power is that it is inexhaustible, so it will never run out.

2 disadvantage / biomass / produces / greenhouse gases

____

3 drawback / biomass / large areas / land / needed

____

4 benefit / hydropower / energy / stored / used / needed

____

5 disadvantage / geothermal / available / certain places

____

COHERENCE

SKILLS

When writing, it is important to make the relationship between different ideas in a text clear to a reader. The ideas should flow in a logical way. This is called *coherence*, and it makes your writing easier for the reader to follow. For example, if you are trying to show how two things are similar or different, that intention should be clear. If you are referring back to an idea already presented, the reader should understand that clearly. Some words you can use to make your writing coherent are:

1 **Pronouns which refer back to an idea already introduced:** *they, them, it, one*, etc.
There are many **types of renewable energy**. **They** are better for the environment than fossil fuels.

2 **Determiners:** *this, that, these, those*, etc.
Solar power is a sustainable type of energy. **This** characteristic makes it attractive for those living in sunny places.

3 **Conjunctions and connectors:** *however, therefore, in contrast, although*, etc.
Geothermal energy does not cause pollution. **However**, it is expensive to install.
Reusing things is efficient and uses very little energy. **Therefore**, it is a viable alternative to recycling.

4 **Transition words and phrases:** *for example, in the same way, still*, etc.
There are some dangers to hydropower. **For example**, the turbines might harm aquatic wildlife.
It can be expensive or time-consuming to recycle rubbish. **Still**, the benefits are clear.

2 Read the paragraph and complete the text with the words from the box.

PLUS

for example	however	in the same way	they (×2)	this

People have different attitudes about alternative energy sources. (1)__________ , some people welcome the construction of wind turbines in their towns and cities. Others, (2)__________ , think that (3)__________ are undesirable. For (4)__________ second group of people, turbines are noisy and unattractive. (5)__________ that some people think hydropower dams are harmful to river environments, people who are against wind turbines think that (6)__________ ruin natural landscapes and pose dangers to local birds.

3 Read the sentences and write a coherent paragraph using all the information. Use Exercise 2 to help you.

1 Turbines and hydropower plants both change the landscape of an area.
2 Some think that they are important sources of alternative energy.
3 Fossil fuel use has been linked to global warming.
4 Some people are more concerned about using fossil fuels than other people are.
5 Some people think it is more important to save money than to reduce global warming.
6 Alternative energy production facilities can be expensive to construct.

____

____

____

____

____

____

WRITING TASK

Explain the advantages and disadvantages of three types of renewable energy and decide which would work best in your country.

PLAN

1 Look back at your notes in Critical thinking. Review the ideas you came up with about different types of renewable energy. Use your ideas to complete the essay outline below.

introductory paragraph: thesis statement	
point 1 (energy type 1): description advantage(s) disadvantage(s)	
point 2 (energy type 2): description advantage(s) disadvantage(s)	
point 3 (energy type 3): description advantage(s) disadvantage(s)	
concluding paragraph: your preferred option and why	

2 Refer to the Task checklist on page 144 as you prepare your essay.

WRITE A FIRST DRAFT

3 Write a first draft of your essay. Write 350–400 words.

REVISE

4 Use the Task checklist to review your essay for content and structure.

TASK CHECKLIST	✔
Did you follow the five-paragraph essay structure?	
Did you describe each type of energy (its advantages and disadvantages) sufficiently?	
Did you explain how each energy type could or could not be used in your country, and what the impact would be?	
Did you explain which option would work best in your country and why?	

5 Make any necessary changes to your essay.

EDIT

6 Use the Language checklist to edit your essay for language errors.

LANGUAGE CHECKLIST	✔
Did you use appropriate subject-specific language?	
Did you spell any energy collocations correctly?	
Did you use commas and relative pronouns appropriately in relative clauses?	
Did you use some of the phrases to introduce advantages and disadvantages presented in this unit?	
Did you use devices to make your writing coherent?	

7 Make any necessary changes to your essay.

OBJECTIVES REVIEW

1 Check your learning objectives for this unit. Write *3*, *2* or *1* for each objective.

3 = very well   2 = well   1 = not so well

I can …

watch and understand a video about wind power.	______
work out meaning from context.	______
evaluate benefits and drawbacks.	______
organize ideas for an essay.	______
use defining and non-defining relative clauses.	______
introduce advantages and disadvantages.	______
make academic writing coherent.	______
write an advantages and disadvantages essay.	______

2 Use the *Unlock* Digital Workbook for more practice with this unit's learning objectives.

UNLOCK ONLINE

WORDLIST

address (v) ⊙	diminish (v)	resistant (adj) ⊙
adopt (v) ⊙	generate (v) ⊙	secure (v) ⊙
alarming (adj)	inexhaustible (adj)	universal (adj) ⊙
aquatic (adj)	initial (adj) ⊙	urgent (adj)
consult (v)	instigate (v)	utilize (v)
contest (v) ⊙	offshore (adv)	vital (adj) ⊙
deliver (v) ⊙	omit (v)	

⊙ = high-frequency words in the Cambridge Academic Corpus

LEARNING OBJECTIVES	IN THIS UNIT YOU WILL ...
Watch and listen	watch and understand a video about an art district in Beijing.
Reading skill	scan to find information.
Critical thinking	understand and evaluate analogies.
Grammar	paraphrase quotations; use substitution; use ellipsis.
Academic writing skills	write arguments, counter-arguments and refutations.
Writing task	write an argumentative essay.

ART AND DESIGN

UNIT 7

UNLOCK YOUR KNOWLEDGE

Work with a partner. Discuss the questions.

1 Do you like art and design? If so, what media (e.g. painting, music, architecture, fashion) do you like?
2 Are you artistic? If so, what kinds of artistic activities do you like doing?
3 Look at the photo. Would you call this art? Why / Why not?
4 Are art and design important for a country's economy? Why / Why not?

PLUS

WATCH AND LISTEN

PREPARING TO WATCH

ACTIVATING YOUR KNOWLEDGE

1 Work with a partner and answer the questions.

1 Where can you find art, either in your own home city or town, or in a city you have visited?
2 Can you find art outside of museums? Where?
3 What happens to older buildings in your city? Are they usually knocked down, or are some used for a different purpose?
4 What are some examples of old buildings that have a new function?

PREDICTING CONTENT USING VISUALS

2 Look at the pictures from the video. Discuss the questions with a partner.

1 Where do you think these pictures were taken?
2 How are these places different from where you usually find art?
3 Do you consider the pieces in the video art? Why / Why not?

GLOSSARY

state-run (adj) operated by the government

present a ... face (phr) give a ... impression

mainstream arts scene (phr) the places and ways in which well-known artists usually work and exhibit their work

struggling artists (n) artists who are working hard but whose work is not well known

WHILE WATCHING

UNDERSTANDING MAIN IDEAS

3 ▶ Watch the video. Which sentence best represents the main idea of the video?

1 Art Zone 798 hosts art exhibitions, film festivals, fashion shows, and theatre productions.
2 Art Zone 798 is a popular attraction today but soon another popular space will replace it.
3 Art Zone 798 began as a work space for struggling artists and is now a major arts centre.

SUMMARIZING

4 ▶ Watch again. Complete the summary.

Years ago, Art Zone 798 was a [1]____________________ . In the 1990s, after the buildings were abandoned, [2]____________________ began to move in. It was the perfect space for the [3]____________________ that many of these artists created. Many different kinds of artists worked at Art Zone 798, including [4]____________________ , fashion designers, photographers and film directors. Soon, more well-known artists began to display their work there, and the centre became [5]____________________ with tourists and local visitors. In addition to the art work, there are services for visitors, including [6]____________________ . Struggling artists can no longer [7]____________________ in Art Zone 798. They have moved to [8]____________________ .

MAKING INFERENCES

5 Circle the statements you can infer from the video. Discuss your answers with a partner.

1 The government opposed the artists' centre when it began in the 1990s.
2 It is possible for some artists to earn a good income today in Beijing.
3 It may still be difficult for some artists to earn enough money in Beijing.
4 There are many other centres like Art Zone 798 in Beijing.

DISCUSSION

6 Discuss the questions with your partner. Compare your answers with another pair.

1 Would you like to visit Art Zone 798? Why / Why not?
2 Have you visited an art centre like this at home or in another country? What was it like?
3 Do you think there should be special spaces where struggling artists can work and show their work? Should the government support the space? Why / Why not?

READING

READING 1

PREPARING TO READ

UNDERSTANDING KEY VOCABULARY

1 You are going to read a magazine article about the nature of art. Read the definitions. Complete the sentences with the words in bold.

> **aesthetic** (adj) relating to the enjoyment or study of beauty, or showing great beauty
> **conceptual** (adj) based on ideas or principles
> **contemporary** (adj) existing or happening now
> **distinction** (n) a difference between similar things
> **established** (adj) generally accepted or familiar; having a long history
> **notion** (n) a belief or idea
> **significance** (n) importance

1. A sculpture in which the artist's main idea or message is considered more important than the technique can be called __________ art.
2. The new museum in town has a lot of __________ appeal. The exterior of the building is very beautifully designed.
3. It is common these days to prefer __________ architecture, but I like the classic, old homes in my neighbourhood.
4. In art class we learned the __________ between fine art and applied art.
5. It is now well __________ that Pablo Picasso was one of the great artists of the twentieth century.
6. Art historians often explain the __________ of very famous works of art and how they may have influenced our society.
7. Many people share the __________ that the term 'art' also applies to things like car and video game design.

PREDICTING CONTENT USING VISUALS

2 Read the descriptions (1–4) and match the artists to the photographs (a–d) of their work.

1 **Andy Warhol:** An artist who was famous for his colourful paintings of ordinary objects such as soup tins. ______
2 **Damien Hirst:** A radical British artist who famously used dead animals in his work. ______
3 **Marcel Duchamp:** An early twentieth-century French artist who changed what people thought of sculpture. ______
4 **Yayoi Kusama:** A Japanese artist famous for her use of bright colours and dots. ______

a

b
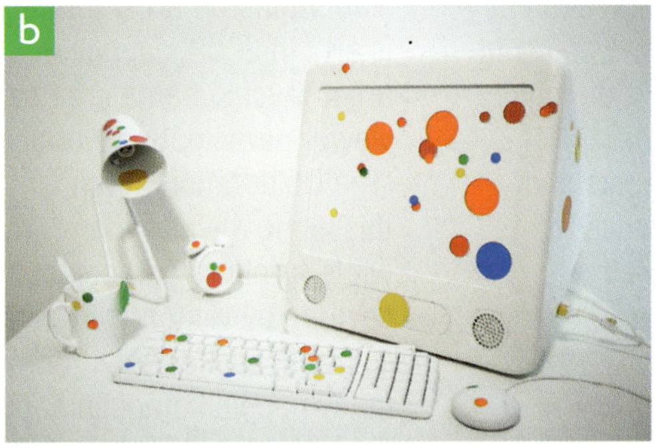
c

d

WHILE READING

SKILLS

Scanning to find information

Scanning is a reading technique used to look for specific information in a text. If you know what information you want from a text, you do not need to read it all. Just move your eye quickly down the page looking for the key words related to the information you want. When you find the information, you can just read that part in detail.

SCANNING TO FIND INFORMATION

3 Scan the magazine article on page 152 and put the artists in the order in which they are mentioned.

a Yayoi Kusama ______
b Damien Hirst ______
c Marcel Duchamp ______
d Andy Warhol ______

ALL THAT ART IS

1

What is art? This question has puzzled philosophers and great thinkers for centuries. In fact, there is disagreement about exactly what art is. Most of us would agree that Leonardo da Vinci's *Mona Lisa* is art, but what about a video game? One dictionary definition states that art is 'making objects, images or music, etc. that are beautiful or that express certain feelings'. This, however, could be regarded as too broad a definition. There are actually a number of different categories of objects and processes under the umbrella term of *art* which can be explored.

2

Art is typically divided into two areas: fine art (such as painting, sculpture, music and poetry) and applied art (such as pottery, weaving, metalworking, furniture making and calligraphy). However, some claim that the *art* label can also be attached to car design, fashion, photography, cooking or even sports. Fine art is categorized as something which only has an **aesthetic** or **conceptual** function. This point was made over a thousand years ago by the Greek philosopher Aristotle, who wrote, 'The aim of art is to represent not the outward appearance of things but their inward **significance**'. He noted that artists produced objects, drama and music which reflected their emotions and ideas, rather than just trying to capture a true image of nature. Andy Warhol, the American artist famous for his Pop Art in the 1960s, once said, 'An artist produces things that people don't need to have'. This is the **distinction** between fine and applied art. Applied arts require an object to be functional as well as beautiful.

3

In the twentieth century, artists began to challenge the **established** idea of art. The French artist Marcel Duchamp changed people's **notion** of what sculpture was, for example, by mounting a bicycle wheel upside down on a stool in 1913 and calling it art. Duchamp said, 'Everything an artist produces is art'. In 2002, Japanese artist Yayoi Kusama created a viewer participation work called 'The Obliteration Room'. In this work, a white room, with white furniture and objects, is covered by visitors with many colourful sticker dots. Today, many people complain about the lack of skill in the production of conceptual artistic objects. Some **contemporary** artists use assistants to produce all their art for them. British artist Damien Hirst claims that as long as he had the idea, it is his work. He has compared his art to architecture, saying, 'You have to look at it as if the artist is an architect, and we don't have a problem that great architects *don't* actually build the houses'.

4

Despite a hundred years of modern art, fine art is still regarded as a preserve of the wealthy. Hirst's works, for example, sell for millions of dollars. Even so, we can see examples of art all around us which are not expensive. Many towns and cities have public art which can be enjoyed by all. Some museums, like the National Art Museum of China in Beijing, are free. Others are free for children and students. Street art is also popular in different neighbourhoods around the world. One British artist, Banksy, has become world-famous for unauthorized[1] works of art painted on building walls. These can be viewed at no charge by anyone who knows where to look for them.

5

Art anthropologist Ellen Dissanayake, in the book *What is Art For?* offers one intriguing function of art: 'the heightening of existence'. In other words, art makes our ordinary, everyday lives a little more special. This notion may not apply to all art, but perhaps we can agree that it is a good goal towards which all artists should reach.

[1]**unauthorized** (adj) without official permission

Sweeping It Under the Carpet by Banksy

4 Read the magazine article again. Write *T* (true), *F* (false) or *DNS* (does not say) next to the statements. Then correct the false statements.

READING FOR DETAIL

_____ 1 The writer feels that the dictionary definition of *art* is too wide.

____

_____ 2 Metalworking is an example of fine art.

____

_____ 3 Some people argue that sports are a type of art.

____

_____ 4 Aristotle was the first to say that art should be affordable for all.

____

_____ 5 Andy Warhol invented Pop Art.

____

_____ 6 'Art for art's sake' refers to applied art.

____

_____ 7 Duchamp's bicycle wheel was sold at an art exhibition for a very high price.

____

_____ 8 Damien Hirst produces all his own art.

____

READING BETWEEN THE LINES

MAKING INFERENCES

5 Which of the artists mentioned in the article would probably have these opinions? Write the names of the artists.

1 It is the idea of the work of art that is most important.
____
2 Art isn't functional. _______________
3 Everything an artist makes can be considered art.
____
4 A building wall can be used like a canvas. _______________
5 It does not matter if the artist doesn't actually make the work of art.
____
6 Everyone can be part of the creative process. _______________

DISCUSSION

6 Work with a partner. Discuss the questions.

1 What do you think is the main purpose of art? Does it need to have a purpose, or can it just be beautiful?
2 Do you think car design should be classified as art? What about graffiti? Explain your answer.
3 Which of the artists in the text do you agree with? Why?

PLUS

READING 2

PREPARING TO READ

USING YOUR KNOWLEDGE

1 You are going to read an essay about photography. Work in pairs. Discuss which of the activities in the box you think are considered art.

computer games	cooking	drawing	fashion
football	gardening	sculpture	photography

UNDERSTANDING KEY VOCABULARY

2 Read the sentences and choose the best definition for the words in bold.

1 Critics **perceived** him to be an especially good painter of real-life situations.
 a thought of in a particular way b misunderstood
2 A camera, unlike a person's hand, is a **mechanical** device.
 a related to fixing equipment b related to machines
3 This artist uses many different **mediums**, such as chalk, oil, paint and pencil.
 a materials used to create art b characteristics of art
4 The artist uses a **sophisticated** 3D printer to create perfectly identical plastic models of real people. The models show great detail from the wrinkles in people's faces to the folds in their clothing.
 a basic and simple b highly developed and complex
5 News reporting, unlike other kinds of writing, is expected to be **objective** and not based on someone's opinion.
 a based on facts and reality b focused on real objects
6 Although I do not think Banksy has the right to paint on buildings without permission, I do **acknowledge** that his work is very imaginative.
 a agree; admit something is true b make a guess about something
7 I prefer sculptures that show something I can recognize rather than **abstract** ones.
 a detailed b not of real things or people
8 The splash of white paint across the painting might look like an accident, but the artist placed it there **deliberately**.
 a intentionally b dangerously

PLUS

WHILE READING

SCANNING TO FIND INFORMATION

3 Quickly scan the essay opposite. In which paragraphs are these points discussed?

1 The concept that fine art is one thing and photography is another. ______
2 Photography is more objective than other kinds of art. ______
3 Some photographers are more vocal about calling themselves artists. ______
4 Photography is a means of producing art, but it's not always art. ______

PHOTOGRAPHY AS ART

1 The production of fine art is the use of skill and imagination to create aesthetic objects or experiences which can be shared with other people. Photography is thought by some to be a form of fine art because it is made using the same critical and creative process that a painter or sculptor would use. It seems clear, however, that there is a significant difference between creating images by hand – using paint, clay or other tools – and pointing a **mechanical** device at something interesting and clicking. Although photography does have some features in common with other kinds of art, it cannot be said that photography is unquestionably art.

2 It is true that photography can be appreciated on the same level as other recognized forms of visual art. Sometimes decisions involved in creating a photograph are similar to those made by any other artist. A photograph is not always just a record of the world, but a **deliberately** created image with its own artistic features. Ansel Adams, the American photographer, commented on this point when he noted that *take* is not the right verb for a photograph. Instead, he said, one *makes* a photograph. To this end, there is a growing trend for photographers to call themselves artists. However, we cannot ignore the fact that artists can sell their pieces in the higher-priced, fine-art markets, whereas photographers cannot. A photograph by German artist Andreas Gursky, for example, recently sold for almost $4.5 million. No one would likely pay that much for a photograph unless the photographer presented himself as an artist.

3 Although some photography can be **abstract**, most photographs are basically **objective** records of a particular place at a particular time. Certainly we can appreciate a beautiful photograph when we see one, but any beauty that is **perceived** in the picture comes from the time and place where it was taken, and it is not the creation of the photographer. Also, **sophisticated** and expensive equipment often plays a greater role in the success of a photograph than the photographer's creativity. Even some of the greatest photographers **acknowledge** that there is a limit to the amount of influence they can have on a final product. Henri Cartier-Bresson, the famous French photographer, admitted that luck was the most important factor. Finally, photography is so widely used for practical functions that have little or nothing to do with art, such as police work, advertising and news reporting, that it cannot claim to be made for aesthetic purposes alone.

4 People have argued whether photography is art ever since the first photographers shared their work. A photographer may make the same aesthetic choices as a fine artist: subject matter, lighting, colour or even a theme or message. However, cameras can also be purely functional tools, capturing visual records and presenting information. Photography is a **medium** that can be used to make art, but that does not mean that all photography is art.

READING BETWEEN THE LINES

MAKING INFERENCES

4 Read the essay again. Answer the questions.

1 Which statement would the author of the article agree with most?
  a Photography is never art.
  b Photography shares some things in common with other art forms.
2 Why does the author mention the high selling price of the Andreas Gursky photograph?
  a to imply that photographers may call themselves artists to make more money
  b to show that even if it is not art, photographs are valuable
3 Why does the author paraphrase Henri Cartier-Bresson?
  a because it indirectly supports the thesis
  b to show that some photographers disagree with him

UNDERSTANDING PARAPHRASE

5 Match the paraphrases (a–e) to the original statements (1–5).

Original statements

1 ... any beauty that is perceived in the picture is the beauty of the time and place where it was taken, and it is not the creation of the photographer. ______
2 ... there is a significant difference between creating images by hand – using paint, clay or other tools – and pointing a mechanical device at something interesting and clicking. ______
3 ... photography is so widely used for practical functions that have little or nothing to do with art, such as police work, advertising and news reporting, that it cannot claim to be made for aesthetic purposes alone. ______
4 ... he noted that *take* is not the right verb for a photograph. Instead, he said, one *makes* a photograph. ______
5 ... no one would likely pay that much for a photograph unless the photographer presented himself as an artist. ______

Paraphrases

a Since photography is frequently used for non-artistic purposes, it cannot be considered art.
b People are willing to pay a lot of money for a photograph which is perceived as art.
c Art cannot be created by a machine.
d The aesthetic value of a photograph comes from the natural world, not from the skill of the person holding the camera.
e Photography requires artistic input.

6 Match the opinions (1–5) to the people (a–e).

MAKING INFERENCES

Opinions

1 There's no reason for a great photograph to be any cheaper than a great painting. ______
2 Even a child could take a great picture of that view. ______
3 There's a lot more skill to making a picture than just pointing a camera at something and clicking. It's something that I create. ______
4 Most of us would just walk by and not notice something that could make a fabulous photo. And even if we did notice we probably wouldn't know how to take a photo that would stir other people's feelings. ______
5 Sometimes you just see something that will make a great picture and the light is perfect and you have your camera with you. At other times, nothing seems to be right. ______

People

a Ansel Adams
b Henri Cartier-Bresson
c Andreas Gursky
d The author of the essay
e Someone who believes photography is art

DISCUSSION

SYNTHESIZING

7 Work with a partner. Use ideas from Reading 1 and Reading 2 to discuss the following questions.

1 Look at the five statements in Exercise 6. What is each statement saying? Which do you agree with? Which do you disagree with?
2 Do you agree with the author's thesis 'It cannot be said that photography is unquestionably art'? Why / Why not?
3 Can a photograph ever be worth as much as a painting?
4 In Reading 1, the author mentions 'the heightening of existence' as one of the functions of art. Do you think photographs can achieve this? Why / Why not?

PLUS

LANGUAGE DEVELOPMENT

PARAPHRASING QUOTATIONS

GRAMMAR

One very important skill in academic writing is *paraphrasing*. Paraphrasing means putting someone else's ideas or quotations into your own words without changing the meaning. When you do this, you must cite the original source. Paraphrasing is used by writers to avoid *plagiarism* (using another person's ideas or work and pretending that it is your own) and to avoid including too many direct quotations.

Here are four techniques you can use to paraphrase:

1 Use reported speech – explaining someone else's opinion without using the same words by using reporting verbs such as *admit, state, say, feel, insist, believe, point out, emphasize, maintain, deny, suggest* and *theorize.*
'Of course, it's all luck.' – Henri Cartier-Bresson
Henri Cartier-Bresson, the famous French photographer, **admitted** that luck was the most important factor.

2 Use synonyms or antonyms for key words.
Henri Cartier-Bresson admitted that luck was a **significant component**.

3 Change the part of speech of some words
Henri Cartier-Bresson made an **admission** that luck was important.

4 Change the sequence of the ideas in a sentence
Luck was important, according to Henri Cartier-Bresson.

Notice how all of these strategies are used in the paraphrase below.

Original quote: 'The chief enemy of creativity is good sense.' – Pablo Picasso
Paraphrase: Pablo Picasso felt that doing things in the usual, sensible way was the main obstacle to imaginative art.

PLUS

1 Read the quotations and write sentences paraphrasing them. Your paraphrase should include the suggested language.

'A picture is worth a thousand words.' – Napoleon Bonaparte (use the verb *explain*)
Napoleon Bonaparte explained that a picture could tell us the same as a thousand words could.

1 'A picture is a poem without words.' – Horace
(use the reporting verb *pointed out* and a synonym phrase for *poem*)

____

2 'Creativity takes courage.' – Henri Matisse
(use the reporting verb *felt* and an antonym for *courage*)

____

3 'The painter has the universe in his mind and hands.' – Leonardo da Vinci
(use the reporting verb *state* and sequence the ideas differently)

____

2 Paraphrase the quotations using the strategies given opposite.

1 'Creativity is the power to connect the seemingly unconnected.' – William Plomer ____

____

2 'I fight pain, anxiety and fear every day, and the only method I have found that relieves my illness is to keep creating art.' – Yayoi Kusama

____

____

3 'Art enables us to find ourselves and lose ourselves at the same time.' – Thomas Merton ____

____

VOCABULARY FOR ART AND DESIGN

3 Read the definitions. Complete the sentences with the best adjective.

abstract (adj) not of real things or people
avant-garde (adj) relating to ideas and styles which are very original and modern
decorative (adj) made to look attractive
expressive (adj) showing what somebody thinks or feels
figurative (adj) showing people or things in a similar way to real life
lifelike (adj) looks very real
monumental (adj) very big
moving (adj) causing strong feelings of sadness or sympathy

1 The __________ bronze sculpture weighs seven tons.
2 It was a(n) __________ performance which left many people in tears.
3 I think art is purely __________ . It is only there to look nice.
4 The tiger sculpture was so __________ that people were a little scared by it.
5 Her work was very __________ ; her ideas took years for people to accept as normal.
6 __________ art can look easy to produce because there are no realistic images.
7 He was interested in __________ art and produced many realistic portraits of people.
8 The paint was applied quickly to the picture in a(n) __________ and emotional way.

a lifelike sculpture

a figurative drawing

PLUS

WRITING

CRITICAL THINKING

At the end of this unit, you will write an argumentative essay. Look at this unit's writing task below.

> Fashion, cooking and video games have all been likened to fine art. Choose *one* of these and discuss whether it should be considered fine art, comparable to painting or sculpture.

ANALYZE

1 Go back to Reading 2 and find examples where the author has a particular opinion, presents an opinion which is different and then explains why the other side is wrong. Complete the table.

paragraph 1 argument: It cannot be said that photography is unquestionably art.	argument against author's opinion: Photography does have features in common with other kinds of art.	why the other side is wrong: Pointing a mechanical device at something interesting and pushing a button is not enough to be 'art'.
paragraph 2 argument:	argument against author's opinion:	why the other side is wrong:
paragraph 3 argument:	argument against author's opinion:	why the other side is wrong:

SKILLS

Understanding and evaluating analogies

An *analogy* is a comparison between two things, often used to help explain a principle or idea. They might seem to have no clear relationship, but by focusing on particular factors, interesting similarities can be identified. An example might be how a doctor and a detective approach their work in similar ways – they are both looking for causes which are not immediately obvious.

2 Read the quotations that use analogies. Circle whether they support or challenge the idea that fashion, cooking or video games are fine art.

UNDERSTAND

1 'Unlike art, fashion rarely expresses more than the headlines of history'. – Alice Rawsthorn	support / challenge
2 'Video games are a unique form of artistic expression through what I call the "three voices": the voice of the designer or artist, the voice of the game and its mechanics and the voice of the player'. – Chris Melissinos	support / challenge
3 'The same amount of artistic expression goes into clothes, a piece of pottery or a painting'. – Zandra Rhodes	support / challenge
4 'For most gamers, video games represent a loss of those precious hours we have available to make ourselves more cultured, civilized and empathetic'. – Roger Ebert	support / challenge
5 Cooking 'doesn't involve the sense of transmission of human emotion in the way that the arts at their highest do'. – Denis Dutton	support / challenge
6 'The art of cooking: it's when you mix craftsmanship at the highest level with creativity'. – Éric Ripert	support / challenge

3 Complete the sentences. Give reasons for your answers.

EVALUATE

1 I *agree* / *disagree* with Zandra Rhodes's argument that the same amount of artistic expression goes into clothing, pottery and paintings because clothes have to be practical enough to wear.

2 I *agree* / *disagree* with Éric Ripert when he says cooking is the mixture of great craftsmanship with creativity because ______________________.

3 I *agree* / *disagree* with Roger Ebert, who argued that video games make us less civilized and empathetic, because ______________________.

4 I *agree* / *disagree* with Denis Dutton, who suggests that cooking doesn't involve the expression of human emotion in the way that other forms of art do, because ______________________.

5 I *agree* / *disagree* with Chris Melissinos's argument that video games are a unique form of artistic expression because ______________________.

6 I *agree* / *disagree* with Alice Rawsthorn's suggestion that fashion is not a true art form because ______________________.

4 Work with a partner. Can you think of any analogies of your own related to the essay question?

CREATE

GRAMMAR FOR WRITING

SUBSTITUTION

GRAMMAR

In academic writing, writers try to avoid repetition when possible. To do this, you can substitute pronouns or other words for nouns or noun phrases. In the sentence below, *this* is used to avoid repetition.

Although many people find cars beautiful, ~~finding cars beautiful~~ **this** does not make cars art.

Here, two pronouns are used in this way:

A work of art can mean different things to different people. **That** is one reason people may find **it** interesting.

1 Read the paragraph and underline the words the author has substituted for the full name of the car.

The Jaguar E-type is probably one of the most famous cars ever produced. The two-seater roadster was the fastest sports car on the market in 1961. The aerodynamic styling of the car is functional yet beautiful. The bullet shape of the E-type contrasts with the body's curves. The machine's most prominent feature is the long, projecting bonnet which contains the powerful engine. The view of the car's shape is as beautiful from the driving seat as it is to the pedestrian. It is easy to see why Enzo Ferrari called it 'the most beautiful car in the world'.

ELLIPSIS

GRAMMAR

Another way to avoid repetition is to leave out some words which have already been mentioned. This is called *ellipsis*.

Some photos have a very clear meaning, but other photos **do not** ~~have a clear meaning~~.

2 Read the paragraph and cross out any words or phrases which can be removed without affecting the meaning of the text. Add any substitutions (such as pronouns) which you think are necessary.

The Scream is the popular name given to each of four paintings of *The Scream* by the artist Edvard Munch who painted *The Scream* between 1893 and 1910. The National Gallery in Oslo holds one painting of *The Scream*, the Munch Museum holds two more paintings of *The Scream*, and the fourth version of *The Scream* sold for $119 million at Sotheby's on 2 May, 2012. To explain the picture of *The Scream*, the artist Edvard Munch wrote in his diary, 'One evening I felt tired and ill. I stopped and looked out over the sea – the sun was setting, and the clouds were turning blood red. I sensed a scream passing through nature; it seemed to me that I heard the scream.'

PLUS

ACADEMIC WRITING SKILLS

ARGUMENTS, COUNTER-ARGUMENTS AND REFUTATIONS

SKILLS

Arguments

In academic writing, it is important to know how to create an effective argument. Using facts, statistics or other kinds of examples will make your argument more convincing. Also, the logic of your argument should be clear. Here is an example of a weak argument:

My cousin Tom is not a good artist because I don't like his paintings.

This argument does not contain any support other than the writer's opinion, and it does not come across as logical. Also, an argument is not a statement of fact – it is something people might disagree with.

My cousin Tom only paints with the colour brown.

Here is an example of a stronger argument:

My cousin Tom's art is not as interesting as Picasso's because Tom always paints the same subject and only uses the colour brown.

This argument uses specific characteristics of the painter's work as support, and it is logical how the writer arrived at his or her opinion.

1 Read each pair of arguments and circle the stronger argument. Explain why you think the other argument is weaker.

1 a Photography is art because 73% of people reported that they have had a 'very emotional response' to a photograph at least once.

b Photography should be considered art because we often see framed photos hanging in people's homes and offices.

____

____

2 a Fashion is art because fashion designers have to make decisions about colour and working with colour is an artistic activity.

b Fashion design uses creativity to make us think or feel emotion just like other types of art.

____

____

3 a Students should study art because, in my opinion, it is fun to create art.

b Students should study art because it has been linked with general success in other subject areas.

____

____

SKILLS

Counter-arguments and refutations

You can strengthen your argument by giving a *counter-argument* and a *refutation*. By presenting the counter-argument, you show that you have considered another point of view. By refuting it with reasons and evidence, you show why the counter-argument does not weaken your own point of view.

Consider this argument:
Photography is a useful medium, but it is not art.

The writer follows this with a counter-argument:
It is true that photography and fine art have some things in common.

Then the writer gives a refutation. Refuting the counter-argument shows the strength of the writer's position:
However, it is still the case that using your hands to create art requires more imagination than using a mechanical device.

The phrase *'However, it's still the case that ...'* indicates the author's argument is still valid.

2 Work with a partner. Complete these counter-argument and refutation sentences in a way which makes sense.

1 Critics of mandatory art education say that art is not as important as academic subjects. Even though that might be true, ____ .

2 Some people believe that art is only for the rich. However, ____ .

3 Opponents of public funding for art ____ .

Nevertheless, public art beautifies our town and enriches our community culture.

3 Read the arguments and counter-arguments and give a refutation.

1 **Argument:** Photography is fine art, just like paintings and sculptures.
Counter-argument: Some people say that photography is not truly fine art because anyone can pick up a camera and take photos.
Refutation: ____

2 **Argument:** Graffiti artists deserve praise and recognition for their work.
Counter-argument: Many critics do not believe that graffiti artists like Banksy should receive praise for their work because it is illegal.
Refutation: ____

4 Work in pairs. Compare your answers and refutations. Do you agree? If not, explain to your partner why you think you are right.

WRITING TASK

Fashion, cooking and video games have all been likened to fine art. Choose *one* of these and discuss whether it should be considered fine art, comparable to painting or sculpture.

PLAN

1 Look back at your notes in Critical thinking. Create an outline for your essay using the following structure for your body paragraphs.

Body paragraph 1: Evidence in favour of one position, counter-argument, refutation
Body paragraph 2: Evidence in favour of one position, counter-argument, refutation
Body paragraph 3: Evidence in favour of one position, counter-argument, refutation

2 Refer to the Task checklist below as you prepare your essay.

WRITE A FIRST DRAFT

3 Write your essay. Write 350–400 words.

REVISE

4 Use the Task checklist to review your essay for content and structure.

TASK CHECKLIST	✔
Did you provide strong arguments for your position as well as counter-arguments and refutations for each argument?	
Did you paraphrase information correctly?	

5 Make any necessary changes to your essay.

EDIT

6 Use the Language checklist to edit your essay for language errors.

LANGUAGE CHECKLIST	✔
Did you use substitution and ellipsis where appropriate?	
Did you use vocabulary for art and design?	

7 Make any necessary changes to your essay.

OBJECTIVES REVIEW

1 Check your learning objectives for this unit. Write *3*, *2* or *1* for each objective.

3 = very well 2 = well 1 = not so well

I can ...

watch and understand a video about an art district in Beijing.	____
scan to find information.	____
understand and evaluate analogies.	____
paraphrase quotations.	____
use substitution.	____
use ellipsis.	____
write arguments, counter-arguments and refutations.	____
write an argumentative essay.	____

2 Use the *Unlock* Digital Workbook for more practice with this unit's learning objectives.

UNLOCK ONLINE

WORDLIST

abstract (adj) ⊙
acknowledge (v) ⊙
aesthetic (adj) ⊙
avant-garde (adj)
conceptual (adj) ⊙
contemporary (adj) ⊙
decorative (adj)
deliberately (adv) ⊙
distinction (n) ⊙
established (adj) ⊙
expressive (adj) ⊙
figurative (adj)
lifelike (adj)
mechanical (adj) ⊙
medium (n) ⊙
monumental (adj)
moving (adj) ⊙
notion (n) ⊙
objective (adj) ⊙
perceive (v) ⊙
significance (n) ⊙
sophisticated (adj) ⊙

⊙ = high-frequency words in the Cambridge Academic Corpus

LEARNING OBJECTIVES	IN THIS UNIT YOU WILL ...
Watch and listen	watch and understand a video about a walking group for retired people.
Reading skill	identify evidence in a text.
Critical thinking	draw appropriate conclusions from graphical data.
Grammar	use verb phrases to show cause and effect; use language of prediction; use the first conditional.
Academic writing skills	use numerical words and phrases; interpret graphs and charts.
Writing task	write an analysis essay.

UNIT 8 AGEING

UNLOCK YOUR KNOWLEDGE

Work with a partner. Discuss the questions below.

1 Are elderly people generally respected in your culture? Why / Why not?
2 How is respect or disrespect shown to elderly people in your culture?
3 Has the perception of elderly people in your culture changed over time? In what ways?
4 Look at the photo. What do people do after they stop working in your culture?

PLUS

WATCH AND LISTEN

PREPARING TO WATCH

ACTIVATING YOUR KNOWLEDGE

1 Work with a partner and answer the questions.

1 What do older people you know do to keep busy?
2 How do you think life has changed in the past 20 years for older people?
3 What are some ways older people can keep fit today?

PREDICTING CONTENT USING VISUALS

2 Look at the pictures from the video. Discuss the questions with a partner.

1 What activities are the older people in the first three pictures participating in?
2 Why do you think they are participating in these activities? What benefits might they provide?
3 What activities are the people in the last picture participating in?
4 Are there any benefits to these activities? What are they?

GLOSSARY

fancy kit (n) complicated equipment
Off you go! (phr) You can leave now. / You can get started now.
brisk (adj) quick and energetic
reverse (v) to cause to go in the opposite direction
widows or widowers (n pl) people whose wives or husbands have died

WHILE WATCHING

UNDERSTANDING MAIN IDEAS

3 Watch the video. Choose the statement that best expresses the main idea.

1 A group in England has been walking together for almost 20 years.
2 Walking is better for older people than other forms of exercise.
3 Walking together in a group is good for the health of older people.
4 Walking is an easy and inexpensive form of exercise.
5 Social activities are important for older people.

UNDERSTANDING DETAIL

4 Watch again. For each main idea, write a supporting detail.

1 Even gentle exercise has health benefits.

____

2 Walking is an easy and convenient form of exercise.

____

3 People in the UK are generally not getting enough exercise these days.

____

4 For older people, there are also social benefits of walking together.

____

MAKING INFERENCES

5 Work with a partner. Discuss the questions. Give reasons for your answers.

1 Why do you think people in the UK are getting less exercise now than in the past?
2 Why do you think the Salford walking group has been so successful?
3 Do you think older people are more likely to participate in activities like this than other forms or exercise? Why / Why not?
4 Why do you think the social aspects of the activity have health benefits?

DISCUSSION

6 Work with a partner and answer the questions.

1 Are there activities for older people in your community? Describe them.
2 What exercise groups do you, or could you, participate in now?
3 In addition to exercise, what other ways are there for older people to stay healthy?
4 Would you participate in a group like this one when you retire? Why / Why not?

READING

READING 1

PREPARING TO READ

UNDERSTANDING KEY VOCABULARY

1 Read the sentences and write the words in bold next to the definitions.

1 Social scientists use **demographic** information to understand more about the populations of cities.
2 It is sometimes more difficult for older people to **adapt** to fast-changing technology than it is for younger people.
3 You should ask someone else for help because I don't have time to **undertake** a new project right now.
4 In her **capacity** as head of the hospital, she makes many decisions about the budget and the staff.
5 At my school, some activities are required for all students, but others are **voluntary**.
6 In my **leisure** time, I enjoy working in my garden.

a ___________ (n) a particular position or job; a role
b ___________ (adj) relating to human populations and the information collected about them such as their size, growth, ages and education
c ___________ (n) the time when you are not working or doing other duties
d ___________ (adj) done without being forced or paid to do it
e ___________ (v) to adjust to different conditions or uses
f ___________ (v) to take responsibility for and begin doing something

USING YOUR KNOWLEDGE

2 You are going to read an interview called 'The social and economic impact of ageing'. Use your knowledge to write three facts which might be in the interview.

1 ____
2 ____
3 ____

3 Try to predict the answers to the questions.

1 To what extent has healthcare improved over the last 50 years?
2 Have these improvements been universal, or only in certain countries?
3 What kinds of problems might old people face in today's society?
4 What kinds of problems might a society face if it has more elderly people?
5 What kinds of benefits can an older population bring to society?

WHILE READING

4 Read the interview to check your ideas. If your ideas were different, why do you think that is?

THE SOCIAL AND ECONOMIC IMPACT OF AGEING

In the next instalment of our series on ***demographic*** *changes, we interview Professor Robert Huffenheimer, an expert on the phenomenon of ageing.*

1 What exactly does *ageing* mean?

It means the population in many countries is, on average, getting older. According to a recent United Nations report, in 2050, there will be more people over the age of 60 than children under 16 for the first time in history.

2 What impact is this ageing process likely to have globally?

Well, obviously it is a good thing that people are living longer, but as a result of this, there are a number of issues which have to be dealt with.

3 For example?

In certain countries, an increasing number of older people are living by themselves, often without any relatives living nearby. The UN reports that 40% of the world's older population lives independently. Some older people are simply unable to take care of themselves, and others can only do so if their houses are specially **adapted**. Likewise, they may be unable to go shopping or wash themselves. Consequently, they need someone, perhaps a professional, to help. And, of course, older people need social activities as well.

4 And how are societies adapting to this?

Supermarkets, for example, have introduced more home-delivery services, which have been particularly beneficial for older people. In addition, there has been significant growth in companies providing services which would traditionally have been **undertaken** by relatives. These include private nursing care and 'Meals on Wheels' services, which deliver food to your door. In the USA, for example, Meals on Wheels serves more than 2.4 million elderly people across America, many of whom are living alone or isolated, according to the Urban Institute.

5 Are there any other areas where the impact of ageing can be clearly seen?

Although it is not a problem yet, many governments are worried about the economic impact of an ageing population. Fewer citizens working and paying taxes obviously results in less money for the government to pay for things like health and education. NBC World News recently reported that in Italy, which has Europe's oldest population, people are now living 30 to 40 years beyond retirement. This means that the number of needy pensioners[1] is rising.

6 What advantages can an older population bring?

Countries with a high percentage of young people need to spend a lot of money on education. In contrast, countries with a lower percentage of children have fewer education costs. In more developed countries, older people tend to have more savings and more **leisure** time. In Japan, for example, according to Bloomberg News, the popularity of luxury train travel among older Japanese people has exploded. Consequently, luxury routes are often sold out. Other elderly people may spend more time online or even go back to studying. Of course, older people do have a lot of experience, and if they can, some continue working in a **voluntary capacity** after they retire[2]. This kind of activity adds a lot to society.

[1]**pensioner** (n) a retired person who receives government money for living expenses

[2]**retire** (v) to leave your job or stop working because of having reached a particular age

READING FOR DETAIL

5 Read the interview again. Write *T* (true), *F* (false) or *DNS* (does not say) next to the statements. Then correct the false statements.

_____ 1 Robert Huffenheimer teaches at Columbia University.
____

_____ 2 The average age of the world's population has increased significantly over the last 50 years.
____

_____ 3 Most older people have relatives nearby.
____

_____ 4 There are both benefits and disadvantages for societies with ageing populations.
____

_____ 5 So far, most private companies have ignored the changing demographic situation.
____

_____ 6 Most countries with an older population have much higher education costs.
____

_____ 7 On average, older people spend four hours per day online.
____

_____ 8 Countries can benefit from the skills of retired people.
____

6 Complete the sentences using words from the interview.

1 Specially adapted houses help elderly people who can't __________ __________ __________ themselves.
2 Older people require __________ __________ as well as professional help with shopping and washing.
3 Home deliveries and __________ __________ __________ are commercial services provided for the elderly.
4 Governments are concerned about the __________ __________ of a large number of elderly people in the population who are not working.
5 Older people are free to travel and learn new skills because they have more __________ and __________ __________ .
6 Experienced older people may choose to do work on a __________ basis to help society.

READING BETWEEN THE LINES

SKILLS

Identifying evidence in a text

Writers need to use persuasive language when making an argument, but it is even more important that good evidence is presented. Writers need to be able to justify everything they say. For example, the evidence presented about Italy in the text is supported by statistics from a news source. When you read claims in a text, look for evidence that the writer uses to justify his or her claim.

7 Work with a partner. Discuss the following questions.

1 Professor Robert Huffenheimer cites NBC World News to present two pieces of evidence to support his point. Can you identify them?
2 Huffenheimer cites Bloomberg News to mention the increase in luxury train travel in Japan. What effect does that citation have in the interview?
3 NBC World News and Bloomberg News are both internationally well-known news sources. How might this affect the persuasiveness of using them for support?

DISCUSSION

8 Work with a partner. Discuss the questions.

1 Does your country have an ageing population?
2 What problems do elderly people in your community face?
3 What do you think can be done to ensure that elderly people in society are protected and cared for?

READING 2

PREPARING TO READ

USING YOUR KNOWLEDGE

1 Work with a partner. Discuss the following question.

Some countries have a higher percentage of young people than older people. What problems, impacts and solutions might result from this?

UNDERSTANDING KEY VOCABULARY

2 You are going to read an essay about the effects of a young population on a society. Read the sentences and choose the best definition for the words in bold.

1 In the 1800s, life expectancy was not as well **documented** as it is today.
   a recorded or written down
   b balanced or evened out
   c understood or learned
2 The **median** age in our country is just 22, so our population is young.
   a the age at which people are considered to be 'middle-aged'
   b the middle number or amount in a series
   c the age at which people legally become adults
3 Governments should **allocate** special funds to help elderly people pay for healthcare costs.
   a give something as a share of a total amount, to be used in a particular way
   b make a decision about something
   c take away from the sum total
4 This chart shows the **proportion** of people between the ages of 50 and 65 in EU countries.
   a the total number of something
   b a part or share of the whole
   c an advantage of something
5 In our country, a senior citizen is a person whose age falls in the **range** between age 65 and end of life.
   a the largest amount that is allowed or possible
   b the middle number or amount
   c the amount or number between a lower and upper limit
6 It can be difficult for elderly people to **cope** with the health problems of ageing by themselves, so they often need special assistance.
   a deal with problems or difficulties successfully
   b make a complaint about something
   c forget about something
7 My grandfather receives a monthly **pension** from the company he used to work for.
   a a bill for services
   b a payment for medical costs
   c a sum of money paid regularly to a person who has retired

PLUS

WHILE READING

READING FOR MAIN IDEAS

3 Read the essay. Check your ideas from Exercise 1. How does having a younger overall population affect Saudi Arabia?

What are the impacts of a young population on a society?

1 There is a well-**documented** problem with the ageing of the global population, but there are also areas of the world where demographics are very different. In many parts of the Middle East and North Africa, there is a much higher **proportion** of young people. The Kingdom of Saudi Arabia, a country of over 30 million people, is one such place. This reality has brought special challenges to the Kingdom in a number of different areas such as education, housing and the economy.

2 The population graph shows the population of men and women in Saudi Arabia and their age **ranges** in 2016. The graph shows Saudi Arabia has a very young population. Upon close analysis, it can be seen that about 27% of the population is age 14 and under, and approximately 19% of the total population is between the ages of 15 and 24. The number of Saudis in their mid-twenties to mid-thirties is particularly high, with almost one in five of the total population falling within just this ten-year age range. In the United States the **median** age is 38, in the United Kingdom it is 40, in Italy it is 45 and in Japan it is 47. In contrast, Saudi Arabia is more youthful, as the median age is 27.

3 The high percentage of children and young people leads to high education costs in Saudi Arabia. The focus on education is a high priority for Saudi society. A recent report showed that education receives 25% of the government's annual budget, making the country's education spending one of the highest in the world. As a result of its demographic profile, the government has been leading a university expansion programme to **cope** with the large number of college-aged students moving through the school system every year.

4 This also has an impact on employment opportunities for young people. Youth unemployment could well become the Kingdom's biggest social challenge in the coming years. These days, the unemployment rate for Saudis between the ages of 16 and 29 is 29%. Unless Saudi Arabia's government can provide enough public-sector jobs, or attract more private-sector employers, more budget expenditure will be needed for unemployment benefits.

5 There is a similar challenge in terms of housing, with more demand than supply. This is a particular problem in places such as Jeddah, Saudi Arabia's second-largest city. Jeddah is on the coast, with a mountain range to the east. Because of this, outward expansion is geographically impossible. As a consequence, houses have become more expensive, and young people may be unable to buy their own homes.

6 Although Saudi Arabia faces several challenges in terms of education, employment and housing as a result of its young population, it does not have to cope with the demands of an ageing population. Because the country has relatively fewer old people than the places mentioned earlier, the costs of healthcare and **pensions** are lower. This will allow more funds to be **allocated** to improving the lives of young people.

Saudi Arabia – 2016
Total population: 28,160,273

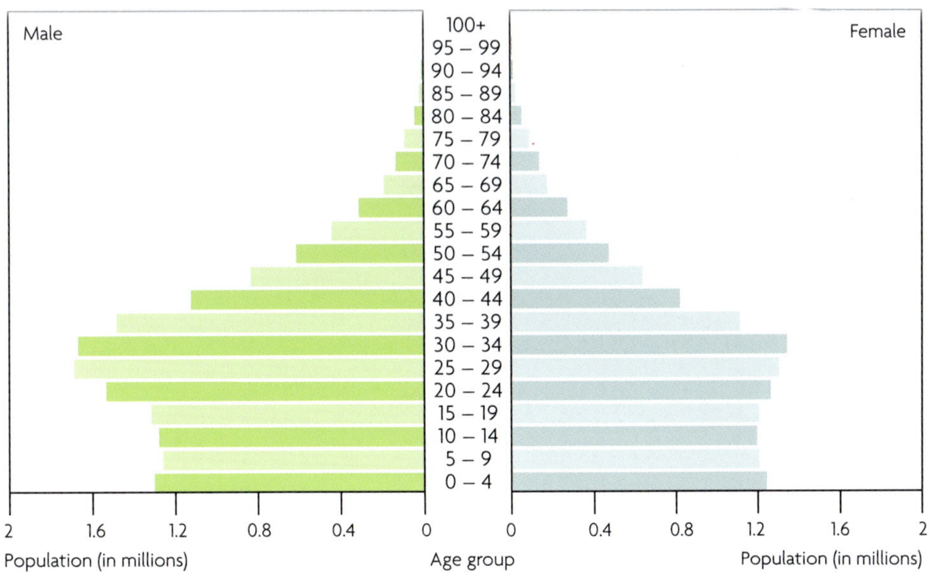

Source: CIA, *The World Factbook*

READING FOR DETAIL

4 Read the essay again. Complete each sentence with a word or number.

1 Saudi Arabia has a very __________ population.
2 Over __________ % of the population is younger than 14.
3 Approximately __________ % of the population is between 15 and 24 years old.
4 The median age for Saudis is __________ , which is 20 years younger than the median age in __________ .
5 Saudi Arabia ranks as one of the top countries in the world for government spending on __________ .
6 In Saudi Arabia there is a lack of employment in both the public and the private __________ .
7 A city which is located between the mountains and the sea has limited space for __________ .

READING BETWEEN THE LINES

WORKING OUT MEANING

5 Work with a partner. Find the words and phrases in the essay and discuss what they mean.

1 upon close analysis
2 expenditure
3 special challenges
4 as a consequence

DISCUSSION

SYNTHESIZING

6 Work with a partner. Use ideas from Reading 1 and Reading 2 to discuss the questions.

1 What are the advantages of a country having a younger population?
2 In a country with income taxation, why is it good to have more workers than retired people?
3 Would it be a good idea to encourage people from countries with a low median age to emigrate and work in foreign countries with ageing populations? Why / Why not?

PLUS

LANGUAGE DEVELOPMENT

ACADEMIC COLLOCATIONS WITH PREPOSITIONS

1 Circle the best preposition to make the collocations.

1 *in / on* brief
2 a range *of / on*
3 focus *on / with*
4 sum *up / on*
5 identify *with / up*
6 *in / with* theory
7 rely *on / with*
8 *on / in* contrast

2 Complete the sentences with the correct phrases and phrasal verbs from Exercise 1.

1 Countries may encounter financial challenges when an increasing number of older people have to ________________ the government for support.
2 Countries with a younger population have high education costs. ________________, those with an older population have to spend more on healthcare.
3 There is a wide ________________ voluntary work opportunities for retired people such as sports coaching, business mentoring, gardening and counselling.
4 There is a tendency to ________________ the problems faced by the elderly, not their valuable contribution to society.
5 ________________, the major problem an ageing population will face is how to fund healthcare.
6 While many strategies may seem to work ________________, when those strategies are put into action, they rarely succeed.
7 It might be difficult for citizens of countries with ageing populations to ________________ the challenges of countries which have a younger population.
8 To ________________, this report's key recommendation is that more educational opportunities should be provided for people over 60.

PLUS

CAUSE AND EFFECT

GRAMMAR

There are simple verb phrases we can use to show the cause and effect of certain actions.

Ageing **results in** greater life experience and wisdom.

Ageing **leads to** greater life experience and wisdom.

Notice how we can also use more complex linkers to show the connection between two sentences.

Retired people in developed countries have more leisure time. **As a result of this**, they can travel more or even go back to studying.

Retired people in developed countries have more leisure time. **Because of this**, they can travel more or even go back to studying.

Retired people in developed countries have more leisure time. **As a consequence**, they can travel more or even go back to studying.

PLUS

3 Complete each sentence (b) with a verb phrase so that it means the same as sentence (a).

1 **a** If a country is ageing, it lowers child education costs.
b An ageing population ______________________________

2 **a** A country that encourages immigration has more young people in it.
b Encouraging immigration ______________________________

3 **a** If the population becomes too old, economics problems may follow.
b An increasingly older population ______________________________

4 Complete the sentences below with your own ideas.

1 Some people never have children. Consequently, ______________________________

2 In some cultures, elderly people commonly live with their adult children. As a result of this, ______________________________

3 It is not always easy for a country to predict how its population will change. Because of this, ______________________________

WRITING

CRITICAL THINKING

At the end of this unit, you will write an analysis essay. Look at this unit's writing task below.

Describe population trends in Japan. Use the data from the graph as evidence to support your claims. Suggest the potential impact on the country if the 2050 projections are correct.

SKILLS

Drawing appropriate conclusions from graphical data

When writing about data, whether in the form of tables, graphs or diagrams, it is important to analyze it carefully, before drawing accurate conclusions. Look for the key messages which the data show, and don't focus on irrelevant information.

ANALYZE

1 Look back at the graph of Saudi Arabia's population in Reading 2 on page 177. Answer the following questions.

1 When was the data in the graph recorded? ___________
2 What is the total population of Saudi Arabia? ___________
3 Are there more people over or under 65 in Saudi Arabia? ___________
4 Does the graph show whether Saudi Arabia has more men or more women? ___________

2 Look at the population graph for Japan and answer the questions.

1 When was the graph created? ___________
2 According to the graph, what is the approximate total population of Japan now? ___________
3 Are there more people over 65 or under 15 in Japan? ___________
4 How is the graph different from the one for Saudi Arabia in Reading 2? What are the reasons for this? ___________________________

____

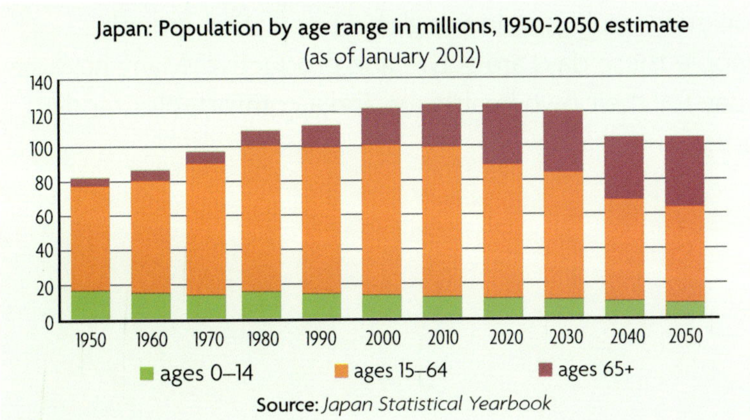

UNDERSTAND

3 Look at the list of demographic ideas below. Work with a partner and find the meaning of three of them. Then, with your class, compare answers and see if together you can work out the meaning of each phrase.

1 youth unemployment
2 housing shortages
3 higher pension costs
4 increased healthcare costs
5 stress on the education system
6 lower consumer spending
7 declining birth rate
8 higher taxes
9 increased emigration
10 increased immigration

APPLY

4 Now identify which one of these could be a problem for a society with an ageing population.

5 Complete the sentences with phrases from Exercise 3.

1 ____________________ are likely in the future because more elderly people will require hospital treatment and help with poor health.
2 If people work for longer periods and retire at an older age, ____________________ may result.
3 ____________________ may be required because there are fewer people of working age paying taxes on their income.
4 Unless the age at which people have to retire increases, there will be ____________________ which taxes will need to pay for.
5 As the population ages, there are fewer people having children. This ____________________ means that the population will actually decrease.
6 In order to replace the lost workforce and to increase levels of taxation, ____________________ may be encouraged by government policies.

EVALUATE

6 Work with a partner. Look at the statements. Which advantage of an older population do you think is the most important? Why?

1 Older people have a great deal of knowledge and experience, which are valuable in the workplace.
2 Older people have more time and money to help their children and grandchildren financially or through helping with childcare and household chores.
3 Older societies result in a slower global population growth.
4 Older people these days are active and productive. Many have savings to help pay for their own healthcare and a comfortable standard of living.

GRAMMAR FOR WRITING

LANGUAGE OF PREDICTION

GRAMMAR

When you describe a graph, you can sometimes predict what might happen in the future based on the trends in the graph. You can use a number of different ways to show that a statement is a prediction.

introduce a strong prediction: *... be likely to, ... be set to, ... be predicted to, ... be expected to, ... be projected to*

Material resource use in the construction sector is expected to reach nearly 90 billion tonnes.

introduces a weak prediction: *... may be*

Young people may be unable to buy their own homes.

introduces a strong negative prediction: *... be unlikely to*

The population is unlikely to get any younger.

1 Match the sentence halves.

1 There is likely
2 There may
3 The number of
4 The population is set
5 We are unlikely to
6 Unemployment is
7 Food prices

a be more wealthy people with more leisure time.
b to be more competition for places at nursing homes in the future.
c projected to increase next year.
d to rise sharply during the next few years.
e young people is expected to remain the same for the foreseeable future.
f are predicted to come down.
g see a sharp rise in immigration.

2 Write sentences with a similar meaning. Include the word in brackets. More than one answer is possible.

1 The population will increase in the future.
____________________ (likely)

2 Oil prices will come down this year.
____________________ (may)

3 Unemployment will remain at the same level in the coming months.
____
____________________ (predicted)

4 The cost of living will rise over the decade.
____________________ (set)

5 There will not be a reduction in the number of schools.
____________________ (unlikely)

THE FIRST CONDITIONAL

GRAMMAR

The first conditional describes possible situations in the future and their likely results using an *if*-clause.

Use the present simple in an *if*-clause to add a condition to an opinion. Use a future verb form in the main clause.

Governments **will need to** address increasing pension costs **if the median age continues** to rise.

Use a comma after the *if*-clause only when it begins the sentence.

If the median age continues to rise, governments **will need to** address increasing pension costs.

In formal writing, you can use more complex linkers to replace *if*, such as *provided that*, *as long as* and *on the condition that*.

Provided that your unemployment benefits claim is approved, you will receive your first payment within two weeks.

You will receive your first payment within two weeks **provided that** your unemployment benefits claim is approved.

3 Circle the best verb forms to complete each sentence.

1 A country *faces* / *will face* problems in the future if the population *ages* / *will age* too much.
2 As long as medical technology *continues* / *will continue* to improve, people *live* / *will live* longer than before.
3 Once my father stops being able to live independently, I *move in* / *will move in* with him on the condition that he *agrees* / *will agree*.
4 If Saudi Arabia *does not create* / *will not create* programmes for the unemployed youth, it *faces* / *will face* a big social challenge.

4 Work with a partner. Rewrite the sentences with a condition using *if* or another linker. Place commas where they are needed.

1 An ageing population results in fewer children.

____

2 More people retiring means fewer people paying income taxes.

____

3 Better education helps a country's young people find good jobs in other countries.

____

4 The population continues to get younger, so the government should prioritize public funds for the young over the ageing.

____

ACADEMIC WRITING SKILLS

NUMERICAL WORDS AND PHRASES

SKILLS

It is important to simplify complex statistical information when writing a description of a graph or chart. To do this, you can use generalizations to introduce the data and specific examples to give details or justify a claim. Numerical words and phrases help you do this.

1 Look at the pie chart about the population of Japan and complete the sentences with words from the box.

Population by age

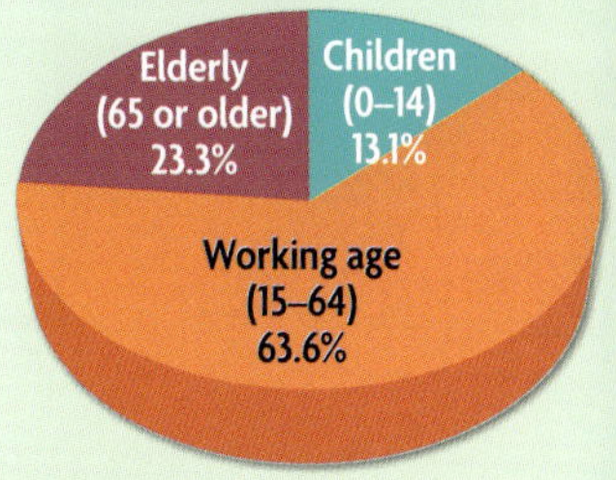

double	half	majority	minority	proportion	quarter	times	triple

1 The overwhelming __________ of Japanese people are of working age.
2 A sizeable __________ (about 23%) are over 65 years old.
3 The number of Japanese people who are of working age is almost five __________ more than those under 14.
4 A significant __________ of the Japanese population is of working age.
5 The percentage of people aged 65 and older is nearly __________ the percentage of children.
6 The percentage of the population who are of working age is nearly __________ that of the elderly.
7 More than __________ the population is of working age.
8 Just under a __________ of the population is over 65.

PLUS

INTERPRETING GRAPHS AND CHARTS

SKILLS

When you write an analysis of information presented on a graph or a chart, keep in mind the following guidelines:

- You should mention the title of the graph or chart, so the reader is clear what the information is referring to.
- You do not need to explain all of the data shown, but you do need to use accurate figures for the data that you refer to.
- You should explain important trends which can be observed in the data.
- You should analyze the data and make predictions (if it is possible to do so).
- Your analysis should stick to the important and relevant trends. Do not include comments which are not related to the main points.

The diagram below shows the global population by age in 1950 and 2000, and projected population figures for 2050. Write an essay describing the information and suggesting what the potential global impact could be if the 2050 projections are correct.

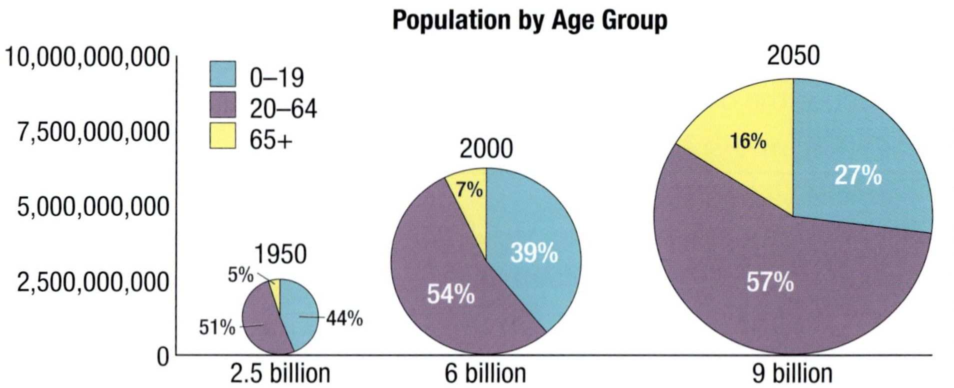

2 Write three sentences about the information in this graph based on the guidelines presented on page 185. Make sure that what you have written is accurately based on the graph.

3 Now look at the following sentences. Which ones would be good to include if you wrote a longer essay? Give reasons for your answers.

1 In 1950, the population was 44% 0-to-19-year-olds, 51% 20-to-64-year-olds and 5% over age 65.

____

2 I think it will be really tough to be a teenager in 2050 because there will be a lot of old people.

____

3 Although there was only a 2% rise in the number of people over 65 between 1950 and 2000, this is projected to rise nearly 10% by 2050.

____

4 This essay will describe the global population by age in 1950 and 2000 and the projected figures for 2050.

____

5 The predicted decrease in the number of young people is likely to have a range of social and economic effects.

____

WRITING TASK

Describe population trends in Japan. Use the data from the graph as evidence to support your claims. Suggest the potential impact on the country if the 2050 projections are correct.

PLAN

1 Look again at the structure of the essay in Reading 2. Write the paragraph numbers from Reading 2 next to the purposes.

_____ Presentation and description of the data from the graphs
_____ Second related challenge
_____ First related challenge
_____ Summary of the challenges but also a mention of an advantage
_____ Third related challenge
_____ Introduction

2 Refer back to the graph in Critical thinking about Japan's population between 1950 and 2050. Write one sentence about what it represents. Paraphrase the language used in the Writing Task.

____

3 Choose three aspects of the data to write about. Consider points which show the general picture or overall trends of the data. Use some of the cause and effect phrases from page 180.

Point 1: ____
Point 2: ____
Point 3: ____

4 Summarize the most interesting or noticeable trend in one sentence.

Main trend: ____

____

5 Think of three important implications of your main argument. A model for Reading 2 is given as an example.

Topic: Saudi Arabia
Main trend: Saudi Arabia's society is very young.
Implication 1: effect on education
Implication 2: effect on the economy
Implication 3: effect on housing

6 Refer to the Task checklist on page 188 as you prepare your essay.

WRITE A FIRST DRAFT

7 Using the essay structure given in Exercise 1 and your notes from Critical thinking and from Exercises 2–5, write the first draft of your essay. Write 350–400 words.

REVISE

8 Use the Task checklist to review your essay for content and structure.

TASK CHECKLIST	✔
Does the structure of your essay follow the structure in Reading 2?	
Did you talk about both the data and its implications?	
Do your examples back up your main trend and its implications?	

9 Make any necessary changes to your essay.

EDIT

10 Use the Language checklist to edit your essay for language errors.

LANGUAGE CHECKLIST	✔
Did you include a sufficient range of appropriate topic-specific and academic language?	
Did you use a range of different numerical words and phrases to interpret the data? Are the phrases accurate?	
Did you use language of prediction including the first conditional, where appropriate?	
Did you use cause and effect phrases?	

11 Make any necessary changes to your essay.

OBJECTIVES REVIEW

1 Check your learning objectives for this unit. Write *3*, *2* or *1* for each objective.

3 = very well   2 = well   1 = not so well

I can …

watch and understand a video about a walking group for retired people.	_____
identify evidence in a text.	_____
draw appropriate conclusions from graphical data.	_____
use verb phrases to show cause and effect.	_____
use language of prediction.	_____
use the first conditional.	_____
use numerical words and phrases.	_____
interpret graphs and charts.	_____
write an analysis essay.	_____

2 Use the *Unlock* Digital Workbook for more practice with this unit's learning objectives.

UNLOCK ONLINE

WORDLIST

a range of (n phr)	focus on (phr v)	pension (n) ⊙
adapt (v) ⊙	identify with (phr v)	proportion (n) ⊙
allocate (v)	in brief (n phr)	range (n) ⊙
capacity (n) ⊙	in contrast (n phr)	rely on (phr v)
cope (v) ⊙	in theory (n phr)	sum up (phr v)
demographic (adj) ⊙	leisure (n) ⊙	undertake (v) ⊙
documented (adj) ⊙	median (adj) ⊙	voluntary (adj) ⊙

⊙ = high-frequency words in the Cambridge Academic Corpus

GLOSSARY

⊙ = high-frequency words in the Cambridge Academic Corpus

Vocabulary	Pronunciation	Part of speech	Definition
UNIT 1			
confuse	/kən'fjuːz/	(v)	to mix up someone's mind or ideas, or to make something difficult to understand
consumption ⊙	/kən'sʌmpʃən/	(n)	the amount of something that someone uses, eats or drinks
continue ⊙	/kən'tɪnjuː/	(v)	to keep happening, existing or doing something, or to cause something or someone to do this
convenience ⊙	/kən'viːniəns/	(n)	the state of being suitable for your purposes and causing the least difficulty
discount ⊙	/'dɪskaʊnt/	(n)	a reduction in the usual price
domestic ⊙	/də'mestɪk/	(adj)	relating to a person's own country
dominant ⊙	/'dɒmɪnənt/	(adj)	more important, stronger or more noticeable than anything else of the same type
ensure ⊙	/ɪn'ʃɔː/	(v)	to make certain that something is done or happens
exclude ⊙	/ɪk'skluːd/	(v)	to prevent someone or something from entering a place or taking part in an activity
exhaust	/ɪg'zɔːst/	(v)	to use something completely
experiment ⊙	/ɪk'sperɪmənt/	(v)	to test or to try a new way of doing something
increase ⊙	/ɪn'kriːs/	(v)	to become larger or greater
inflation ⊙	/ɪn'fleɪʃən/	(n)	a continuing rise in prices in an economy
influence ⊙	/'ɪnfluəns/	(n)	the power to have an effect on people or things, or someone or something which is able to do this

Vocabulary	Pronunciation	Part of speech	Definition
monopoly	/mə'nɒpəli/	(n)	(an organization or group which has) complete control of something, especially an area of business, so that others have no share
multinational	/ˌmʌlti'næʃənəl/	(adj)	operating in different countries
outlet	/'aʊtlet/	(n)	a shop that is one of many owned by a particular company and that sells the goods that the company has produced
refuse	/rɪ'fjuːz/	(v)	to say that you will not do or accept something
relatively	/'relətɪvli/	(adv)	quite good, bad, etc. in comparison with other similar things or with what you expect
remove	/rɪ'muːv/	(v)	to take something or someone away from somewhere, or off something
reputation	/ˌrepjə'teɪʃən/	(n)	the general opinion that people have about someone or something based on their behaviour or character in the past
selling point	/'selɪŋ pɔɪnt/	(n)	a feature that persuades people to buy a product
specialty	/ˌspeʃi'æləti/	(n)	a product that a place is especially known for
study	/'stʌdi/	(v)	to examine something very carefully
supplier	/sə'plaɪə/	(n)	a person or company that provides goods of a particular kind

UNIT 2

Vocabulary	Pronunciation	Part of speech	Definition
alternative	/ɒl'tɜːnətɪv/	(n)	something that is different, especially from what is usual; a choice
aspect	/'æspekt/	(n)	a feature of something
assignment	/ə'saɪnmənt/	(n)	a written essay at university
concrete	/'kɒŋkriːt/	(adj)	based on actual things and particular examples
core	/kɔː/	(adj)	central, basic
core principles	/kɔː prɪnsəpəl/	(n phr)	key values
credible alternative	/'kredəbəl ɒl'tɜːnətɪv /	(n phr)	reliable substitute

Vocabulary	Pronunciation	Part of speech	Definition
degree ⊙	/dɪ'griː/	(n)	a course of study at a college or university, or the qualification given to a student after he or she has completed his or her studies
discipline ⊙	/'dɪsəplɪn/	(n)	a particular area of study
dissertation ⊙	/ˌdɪsə'teɪʃən/	(n)	a long essay of between 8,000 and 12,000 words
distance learning	/'dɪstəns 'lɜːnɪŋ/	(n phr)	general education from online instruction
establishment ⊙	/ɪ'stæblɪʃmənt/	(n)	the act of starting or creating something that will last a long time
evolve ⊙	/ɪ'vɒlv/	(v)	to change or develop gradually
examination ⊙	/ɪgˌzæmɪ'neɪʃən/	(n)	a formal test which students must pass to get a specific qualification
gender gap	/'dʒendər gæp/	(n phr)	the difference in opportunities, attitudes, pay, etc. between men and women
journal ⊙	/'dʒɜːnəl/	(n)	is a quarterly, peer-reviewed collection of research papers
launch	/lɔːntʃ/	(v)	to begin something or introduce a new plan
lecturer	/'lektʃərə/	(n)	is the holder of a research position at a university who also teaches
modern phenomenon	/'mɒdən fə'nɒmɪnən/	(n phr)	recent trend
motivation ⊙	/ˌməʊtɪ'veɪʃən/	(n)	willingness to do something
online degree	/'ɒnlaɪn dɪ'griː/	(n phr)	an academic qualification obtained from online instruction
oriented ⊙	/ɔːrientɪd/	(adj)	directed towards or focused on
plagiarism	/'pleɪdʒərɪzəm/	(n)	when students copy from or do not acknowledge their sources when writing an essay
principle ⊙	/prɪnsəpəl/	(adj)	a basic truth that explains or controls how something happens or works
pursue ⊙	/pə'sjuː/	(v)	to try to do or achieve

Vocabulary	Pronunciation	Part of speech	Definition
semester	/sɪ'mestə/	(n)	one of the two periods into which a year is divided at a college or university
seminar	/'semɪnɑː/	(n)	an occasion when a teacher or expert and a group of people meet to study and discuss something
significant	/sɪg'nɪfɪkənt/	(adj)	important, large or great
significant difference	/sɪg'nɪfɪkənt 'dɪfərəns/	(n phr)	important distinction
specific	/spə'sɪfɪk/	(adj)	relating to one thing and not others; particular
technological advances	/ˌteknə'lɒdʒɪkəl əd'vɑːnsɪz/	(n phr)	developments in technology
term	/tɜːm/	(n)	one of the three periods into which a year is divided at school, college or university
tutor	/'tʃuːtə/	(n)	the person who assumes responsibility for students' academic and personal welfare
under-represented	/ʌndərepri'zentɪd/	(adj)	not given enough presence; in unreasonably lower numbers than others
virtual	/'vɜːtʃuəl/	(adj)	similar to real life but existing in a technological environment
virtual classroom	/'vɜːtʃuəl 'klɑːsruːm/	(n phr)	online course
UNIT 3			
adequate	/'ædəkwət/	(adj)	enough or satisfactory for a particular purpose
adverse	/æd'vɝːs/	(adj)	having a negative or harmful effect on something
burden	/'bɜːdən/	(n)	a duty or responsibility that is hard to bear
chief	/tʃiːf/	(adj)	most important or main
complex	/'kɒmpleks/	(adj)	difficult to understand or find an answer to because of having many different parts

Vocabulary	Pronunciation	Part of speech	Definition
consultation	/ˌkɒnsʌl'teɪʃən/	(n)	a meeting to discuss something or to get advice
contribution	/ˌkɒntrɪ'bjuːʃən/	(n)	an amount of money that is given to help pay for something
controversial	/ˌkɒntrə'vɜːʃəl/	(adj)	causing disagreement or discussion
conventional	/kən'venʃənəl/	(adj)	following the usual practices
drug dependency	/drʌg dɪ'pendənsi/	(n phr)	being unable to function normally without a particular type of medicine
epidemic	/ˌepɪ'demɪk/	(n)	an illness that affects large numbers of people at the same time
fund	/fʌnd/	(v)	to provide money to pay for something
illegal	/ɪ'liːgəl/	(adj)	against the law
labour	/'leɪbər/	(n)	workers, especially people who do practical work with their hands
medical	/'medɪkəl/	(adj)	related to the treatment of illness and injuries
patent	/'peɪtənt/	(n)	the official legal right to make or sell an invention for a particular number of years
physical	/'fɪzɪkəl/	(adj)	connected with the body
precise	/prɪ'saɪs/	(adj)	exact and accurate
preventable illness	/prɪ'ventəbəl 'ɪlnəs/	(n phr)	a disease that can be avoided, often by a person looking after themselves better
professional	/ prə'feʃənəl/	(adj)	having the qualities that you connect with trained and skilled people
proponent	/prə'pəʊnənt/	(n)	a person who supports a particular idea or plan of action
regardless	/rɪ'gɑːdləs/	(adv)	despite; not being affected by something
safety net	/'seɪfti net/	(n phr)	something used to protect a person against possible hardship or difficulty
sedentary lifestyle	/'sedəntəri laɪfstaɪl/	(n phr)	a way of life that does not involve much activity or exercise

Vocabulary	Pronunciation	Part of speech	Definition
substances	/ˈsʌbstənsɪz/	(n)	materials with particular physical characteristics
surgery	/ˈsɜːdʒəri/	(n)	the cutting open of the body to repair a damaged part
symptoms	/ˈsɪmptəmz/	(n)	reactions or feelings of illness that are caused by a disease
treatment	/ˈtriːtmənt/	(n)	the use of drugs, exercise, etc. to improve the condition of a sick or injured person, or to cure a disease
underfunding	/ˌʌndəˈfʌndɪŋ/	(n)	the lack of money provided for something, often academic or scientific research

UNIT 4

Vocabulary	Pronunciation	Part of speech	Definition
casualty	/ˈkæʒjuəlti/	(n)	a person hurt or killed in a serious accident or event
community	/kəˈmjuːnəti/	(n)	the people living in one particular area
criticize	/ˈkrɪtɪsaɪz/	(v)	to express disapproval of someone or something
crucial	/ˈkruːʃəl/	(adj)	extremely important or necessary
devastating	/ˈdevəsteɪtɪŋ/	(adj)	causing a lot of damage or destruction
disaster	/dɪˈzɑːstə/	(n)	something that causes great harm or damage
disrupt	/dɪsˈrʌpt/	(v)	to prevent something from continuing as expected
extreme	/ɪkˈstriːm/	(adj)	the most unusual or the most serious possible
identify	/aɪˈdentɪfaɪ/	(v)	to recognize something and say what that thing is
infrastructure	/ˈɪnfrəˌstrʌktʃə/	(n)	the basic systems and services, such as transport and power, that a country uses to work effectively
issue	/ˈɪʃuː/	(n)	a subject or problem that people are thinking about or discussing
large-scale	/ˌlɑːdʒˈskeɪl/	(adj)	involving a lot of people or happening in big numbers

Vocabulary	Pronunciation	Part of speech	Definition
long-term	/ˌlɒŋ'tɜːm/	(adj)	continuing a long time into the future
maintenance	/'meɪntənəns/	(n)	the work needed to keep something in good condition
major	/'meɪdʒə/	(adj)	more important, bigger or more serious than others of the same type
measure	/'meʒə/	(n)	a method for dealing with a situation
monitor	/'mɒnɪtə/	(v)	to watch and check something carefully over a period of time
policy	/'pɒləsi/	(n)	a set of ideas or a plan for action that a business, government, political party or group of people follow
reduction	/rɪ'dʌkʃən/	(n)	the act of making something smaller in size or amount
rely on	/rɪ'laɪ ˌɔn/	(phr v)	to depend on or trust someone or something
severe	/sɪ'vɪə	(adj)	extremely bad
strategy	/'strætədʒi/	(n)	a long-range plan for achieving a goal
UNIT 5			
amenities	/ə'miːnətis/	(n)	facilities that people enjoy living near, such as libraries, swimming pools and playgrounds
architectural	/ˌɑːkɪ'tektʃərəl/	(adj)	relating to architecture
architecturally	/ˌɑːkɪ'tektʃərəli/	(adv)	in an architectural way
architecture	/'ɑːkɪtektʃə/	(n)	the art and practice of designing and making buildings
civilized	/'sɪvəlaɪzd/	(adj)	having a well-developed way of life and social systems
compromise	/'kɒmprəmaɪz/	(n)	an agreement between two sides who have different opinions, in which each side gives up something it had wanted
conservation	/ˌkɒnsə'veɪʃən/	(n)	the protection of plants, animals and natural areas from the damaging effects of human activity
demonstrate	/'demənstreɪt/	(v)	to show how to do something; to explain

Vocabulary	Pronunciation	Part of speech	Definition
depress	/dɪ'pres/	(v)	to cause someone to feel unhappy and without hope
depressing	/dɪ'presɪŋ/	(adj)	making you feel unhappy and without hope
depressingly	/dɪ'presɪŋli/	(adv)	in a way that makes you feel unhappy and without hope for the future
depression	/dɪ'preʃən/	(n)	the state of feeling very unhappy and without hope for the future
durable	/'dʒʊərəbəl/	(adj)	able to last a long time without being damaged
efficiency	/ɪ'fɪʃənsi/	(n)	the condition or fact of producing the results you want without waste
efficient	/ɪ'fɪʃənt/	(adj)	working or operating quickly and effectively in an organized way
environmental	/ɪn͵vaɪrən'mentəl/	(adj)	relating to the environment
environmentally	/ɪn͵vaɪrən'mentəli/	(adv)	relating to the environment
function	/'fʌŋkʃən/	(n)	a purpose, or the way something works
green belt	/griːn belt/	(n phr)	a strip of countryside round a city or town where building is not allowed
inspiring	/ɪn'spaɪərɪŋ/	(adj)	giving you new ideas and making you feel you want to do something
outskirts	/'aʊtskɜːts/	(n)	the areas which form the edge of a town or city
reflect on	/rɪ'flekt ɒn/	(phr v)	to cause people to think of someone or something in a specified way
relevant	/'reləvənt/	(adj)	related to a subject or to something happening or being discussed
reputation	/͵repjə'teɪʃən/	(n)	the general opinion that people have about someone
responsibility	/rɪ͵spɒnsɪ'bɪləti/	(n)	something that it is your job or duty to deal with
responsible	/rɪ'spɒnsəbəl/	(adj)	to have control and authority over something or someone and the duty of taking care of it, him or her
second-hand	/'sek·ənd'hænd/	(adj)	not new; having been used in the past by someone else

Vocabulary	Pronunciation	Part of speech	Definition
sector	/'sektər/	(n)	a part of society that can be separated from other parts because of its own special character
skyscrapers	/'skaɪˌskreɪpərs/	(n)	very tall modern buildings in cities
structural engineer	/ˌstrʌktʃərəl endʒɪ'nɪər/	(n phr)	a person whose job it is to help build an architect's design
suburban	/sə'bɜːbən/	(adj)	relating to an area on the edge of a large town or city where people who work in the town or city often live
urban sprawl	/'ɜr·bən 'sprɔl/	(n phr)	the spread of a city into the area surrounding it, often without planning
UNIT 6			
address	/ə'dres/	(v)	to give attention to or to deal with a matter or problem
adopt	/ə'dɒpt/	(v)	to accept or begin to use something
alarming	/ə'lɑːmɪŋ/	(adj)	causing worry or fear
aquatic	/ə'kwætɪk/	(adj)	living in, happening in or connected with water
consult	/kən'sʌlt/	(v)	to get information or advice from a person, book, etc. with special knowledge on a particular subject
contest	/kən'test/	(v)	to disagree with
deliver	/dɪ'lɪvə/	(v)	to give
diminish	/dɪ'mɪnɪʃ/	(v)	to reduce or be reduced in size or importance
generate	/'dʒenəreɪt/	(v)	to cause to exist; produce
inexhaustible	/ˌɪnɪg'zɔːstəbəl/	(adj)	in such large amounts that it cannot be used up
initial	/ɪ'nɪʃəl/	(adj)	at the beginning; first
instigate	/'ɪnstɪgeɪt/	(v)	to cause an event or situation to happen
offshore	/ˌɒf'ʃɔː/	(adv)	away from or at a distance from the land
omit	/əʊ'mɪt/	(v)	to skip, to leave out

Vocabulary	Pronunciation	Part of speech	Definition
resistant	/rɪ'zɪstənt/	(adj)	not accepting of something
secure	/sɪ'kjʊə/	(v)	to get something, sometimes with difficulty
universal	/ˌjuːnɪ'vɜːsəl/	(adj)	existing everywhere or involving everyone
urgent	/'ɜːdʒənt/	(adj)	needing immediate attention
utilize	/'juːtəlaɪz/	(v)	to make use of something
vital	/'vaɪtəl/	(adj)	necessary or extremely important for the success or continued existence of something

UNIT 7

Vocabulary	Pronunciation	Part of speech	Definition
abstract	/'æbstrækt/	(adj)	not of real things or people
acknowledge	/ək'nɒlɪdʒ/	(v)	to agree; to admit something is true
aesthetic	/es'θetɪk/	(adj)	relating to the enjoyment or study of beauty, or showing great beauty
avant-garde	/ˌævɑ̃ː'gɑːd/	(adj)	relating to ideas and styles which are very original and modern
conceptual	/kən'septʃuəl/	(adj)	based on ideas or principles
contemporary	/kən'tempərəri/	(adj)	existing or happening now
decorative	/'dekərətɪv/	(adj)	made to look attractive
deliberately	/dɪ'lɪbərətli/	(adv)	intentionally or in a planned way
distinction	/dɪ'stɪŋkʃən/	(n)	a difference between similar things
established	/ɪ'stæblɪʃt/	(adj)	generally accepted or familiar; having a long history
expressive	/ɪk'spresɪv/	(adj)	showing what somebody thinks or feels
figurative	/'fɪgərətɪv/	(adj)	showing people or things in a similar way to real life
lifelike	/'laɪflaɪk/	(adj)	looks very real
mechanical	/mə'kænɪkəl/	(adj)	related to machines
medium	/'miːdiəmz/	(n)	a material used to create art
monumental	/ˌmɒnjə'mentəl/	(adj)	very big

Vocabulary	Pronunciation	Part of speech	Definition
moving	/ˈmuːvɪŋ/	(adj)	causing strong feelings of sadness or sympathy
notion	/ˈnəʊʃən/	(n)	a belief or idea
objective	/əbˈdʒektɪv/	(adj)	based on facts and reality
perceive	/pəˈsiːv/	(v)	to think of in a particular way
significance	/sɪgˈnɪfɪkəns/	(n)	importance
sophisticated	/səˈfɪstɪkeɪtɪd/	(adj)	highly developed and complex
UNIT 8			
a range of	/ə reɪndʒ əv/	(n phr)	a set of similar things
adapt	əˈdæpt/	(v)	to adjust to different conditions or uses
allocate	/ˈæləkeɪt/	(v)	to give something as a share of a total amount, to be used in a particular way
capacity	/kəˈpæsəti/	(n)	a particular position or job; a role
cope	/kəʊp/	(v)	to deal with problems or difficulties successfully
demographic	/ˌdeməˈgræfɪk/	(adj)	relating to human populations and the information collected about them such as their size, growth, ages and education
documented	/ˈdɒkjəməntɪd/	(adj)	recorded or written down
focus on	/ˈfəʊkəs ɒn/	(phr v)	to give a lot of attention to one particular person, subject or thing
identify with	/aɪˈdentɪfaɪ wɪð/	(phr v)	to feel that you can support something
in brief	/ɪn briːf/	(n phr)	lasting only a short time or containing few words
in contrast	/ɪn ˈkɒntrɑːst/	(n phr)	an obvious difference between two or more things
in theory	/ɪn ˈθɪəri/	(n phr)	If something is possible in theory, it should be possible, but often it does not happen in that way
leisure	/ˈleʒə/	(n)	the time when you are not working or doing other duties

Vocabulary	Pronunciation	Part of speech	Definition
median	/ˈmiːdiən/	(adj)	the middle number or amount in a series
pension	/ˈpenʃən/	(n)	a sum of money paid regularly to a person who has retired
proportion	/prəˈpɔːʃən/	(n)	a part or share of the whole
range	/reɪndʒ/	(n)	amount or number between a lower and upper limit
rely on	/rɪˈlaɪ ɒn/	(phr v)	to need a particular thing or the help and support of someone or something in order to continue, to work correctly or to succeed
sum up	/sʌm ʌp/	(phr v)	to make a summary of the main points
undertake	/ˌʌndəˈteɪk/	(v)	to take responsibility for and begin doing something
voluntary	/ˈvɒləntəri/	(adj)	done without being forced or paid to do it

VIDEO SCRIPTS

UNIT 1

China plans revival of Silk Road trade routes

Commentator: We're up in the mountains near the border with Kazakhstan on China's far western frontier. The area we're travelling through is pretty remote, close to the furthest point from an ocean on the planet. This is the land of the old Silk Road where caravans of merchants trekked more than a thousand years ago at the height of China's imperial past. It's now at the heart of the country's plan to rebuild those ancient trading routes over land and by sea in one of the most expensive development projects ever attempted. This is a good place to come to understand the scale of those ambitions. Five years ago, there was almost nothing here. All of this has been built from scratch, including this brand new dry port intended as a key logistics hub for road and rail. Alongside a vast new free trade zone.

Mr Guo has big dreams for this project. He tells me Korgas could be the new Shenzhen or Shanghai.

Guo Jianbin: I think in three or four years, you will see the sky in Korgas will be more blue, and the city will become more beautiful and international trade will play a more key role.

Commentator: This is the 'build it and they will come' approach to infrastructure and trade, build the roads and rail links out into the regions' developing countries and the trade will follow, so the theory goes.

This huge cargo train is lumbering past us now on its way from China to Europe and this is very much the image of the modern Silk Road the Chinese government wants to project. But there's more going on here than just investment in infrastructure. This project is as much about politics as it is about economics.

Ethan Cramer-Flood studies the project for an economic think tank and sees it as being driven primarily by China's domestic economic objectives and its broader geo-political goals.

Ethan Cramer-Flood: This is absolutely first and foremost err ... a soft power initiative where it's clearly err ... China has the leaders ... leadership in Beijing and Beijing envisions the One Belt One Road project as being a significant, maybe the number one most significant part of Xi Jinping's err ... so called 'China dream' and vision of ... of supporting the emergence of China onto the global stage as the next great superpower.

UNIT 2

Disadvantaged children take part in trial of private tutor app

Commentator: GCSE Maths, it's tough enough even when you're in the classroom and the teacher's there to answer your questions. But what about when you're doing your homework and there's no one around who can help? These pupils in Tower Hamlets are trying out a new app. It's giving free instant Maths help to those who might not otherwise be able to afford private tuition.

Peter Kirby: We know that over 90% of teenagers' digital communication is now text-based, so we wanted to design something that would meet them where they were.

Sheikh Fahmida Musarrat: If you, or your Mum or Dad don't know, it's like the next alternative. You don't need to go and look for tutors, and you don't have to like, stay behind in class just to catch up on work.

Commentator: Catching up outside the classroom is extra important these days; in London almost half of secondary school pupils have now received private tuition.

Dr Lee Elliot-Major: The gap between the 'haves' and the 'have-nots' if you like in education is widening, outside the school gate, not just in schools. So we're really concerned about that, and that's why we think that these sorts of agencies that provide tutoring should look at ways at helping those children from poorer backgrounds.

Commentator: Oaklands School here in Tower Hamlets is one of five across the capital now piloting this new app, the others are in Lewisham, Brent, Lambeth and Westminster and the idea is, if it's successful, to roll the app out across the whole of the UK.

Teachers here say they'd welcome anything that helps their pupils get ahead.

Simon Ramsay: Not all of our students can afford private tutors ... erm, and this is a way that circumvents that and allows them to access err ... qualified err ... tutors in their own time so in terms of levelling the play ... playing field err ... yeah it's a great opportunity.

UNIT 3

Robot revolution: robotic surgery is on the rise

Commentator: They don't get tired, their hands don't tremble and their patients make a faster recovery. Robot surgeons are increasingly used in NHS hospitals, but the revolution has only just begun.

Gauthier Gras: It is a sort of see-through vision.

Commentator: Robotic technology will in future give surgeons super-human powers. This probe being developed at Imperial College London not only warns a brain surgeon when they're pressing too hard on delicate tissue, but it also reveals the structures that lie beneath, using scans taken before the operation.

Gauthier Gras: If you're closing in on this aneurysm you'd really want to be aware of the forces that are applied. Err ... it's, it's very easy to ... to apply too much force, and then suddenly rupture it. You're able to warn the surgeon ahead of time to prevent damage.

Commentator: Shrinking technology is allowing scientists to make robotic tools too small to see with the naked eye. These are less than half the width of a human hair, and dexterous enough to move a microscopic ball. It could one day be possible to operate on individual cells at the earliest stage of disease.

Professor Guang-Zhong Yang: The type of robot we are making actually getting smaller and smaller can be actually delivered in the needle form. So therefore, you don't need to make any incisions. So, they can actually follow the err ... curved anatomical pathways, reaching to the side.

Dan Melville: If I think about flicking up lightly, it opens like that.

Commentator: Robotics of a different kind, and for Dan Melville it's life changing.

Dan Melville: So, this is me, err, trying to test it out and see how it goes. This is the first time actually testing it, so, err ... good luck to myself.

Commentator: By tensing his arm muscles he can control his bionic digits, changing his grip to pick up different objects. It's sophisticated technology, but it's being printed in just a few hours, sized to fit and in his choice of colour.

Dan Melville: You can customize it, you can change the colour so if, err ... . a girl wanted black and orange and red, you can have whatever you want and you would just and I ... I personally think it's a fantastic opportunity to just kind of show who you really are on your arm. So, it makes it more personalized for you as well.

Commentator: High-end bionic hands can cost up to £90,000, beyond the reach of the NHS, but Open Bionics hopes to launch its own version by the end of next year, the price of less than £2,000.

Sammy Payne: All of the grip patterns that the advanced bionic hands can do, all of the movements we are replicating and the manufacturing techniques that they're ... they're using, um ... is a very expensive manufacturing process. Whereas we have desktop 3D printers that just print using plastic filaments. I mean you couldn't ... they're worlds apart, the manufacturing methods. Um so that's how we can be so low cost.

Commentator: Patients and surgeons enhanced by robotic technology. We're entering the age of the cyborg.

UNIT 4

Population and water

Narrator: We call our Earth 'the blue planet' because about 70% of the Earth's surface is covered in water. But most of that is in the oceans and seas. Just 2.5% is fresh water, and only 1% of that is available for human use. The rest is locked up in mountain passes and the Earth's polar ice caps. But there's another fact we need to understand about water.

Brian Richter: Well, there's no more water on the planet than there was when life first appeared on Earth. It changes its distribution, there's more water in different parts of the world than there were hundreds or thousands of years ago, but it's still exactly the same amount of water that's been here always.

Narrator: We use over half of all the available fresh water in the world to serve our needs: to transform deserts into fields, to produce energy from rivers and to build cities in some of the driest regions on the planet. But despite our creativity, there are many who have difficulty getting enough of this basic resource.

Brian Richter: More than a billion people on the planet already lack access to safe, clean drinking water. And we know things are going to get more difficult as the population continues to grow. Within the next 20 years, as much as half of the world's population will live in areas of water stress.

Narrator: Many water shortages are the result of poor infrastructure, politics, poverty or simply living in a dry part of the world. But more and more, they are due to increasing populations. Mexico City, for example, benefits from heavy annual rainfall. But its water system is stressed from supplying water to its 20 million inhabitants. The issue is the combination of leaks in the system and the fact that backup reservoirs are running dry. In Mexico City, shops that sell water for people's daily needs are becoming more and more common. But the water we use at home is only a small percentage of the total amount of water we consume. That's because of the huge amounts used by farms and factories.

Brian Richter: We may know where the water out of our tap comes from, but we very seldom know where the water that went into our can of cola or into the shirt that we're wearing on our back, where those goods were produced and how much water it required, and what the consequences were for the natural systems in those areas and for the local communities that are dependent upon that same water.

So for example, the cup of coffee that you may have in the morning requires on the order of 120 litres just to produce the coffee and bring it to your table. A hamburger, 8,000 litres of water, to produce enough water to grow the cotton in my shirt is 3,000 litres as well.

Narrator: The influence of humans on the world's fresh water systems is so significant that it can be seen from space. The Aral Sea, the fresh water lake in central Asia, once covered more than 25,000 square miles. But in the last 40 years, it has lost 90% of its water, with most of it going to support cotton farms. Lake Chad, on the southern side of the Sahara Desert, is now one tenth of its normal size due to drought and overuse. Yet, 30 million people still depend on it.

UNIT 5

Government grants for warmer, cheaper housing

Commentator: Britain's got some of the chilliest buildings in Europe, £1 in every four we spend on heating is wasted due to things like poor insulation. Today the government announced it will extend grants for insulation work like this for warmer, cheaper housing for people who can least afford it.

Gareth Redmond-King: Emissions from homes have started to go up now, and that's a huge problem given the … the scale of the challenge to reduce our emissions by 80% by 2050. Um … so at the current rate of err … improving the energy efficiency of our homes we've calculated it will take us over a hundred years err … to cut emissions from our homes.

Commentator: So, this is the sort of thing campaigners welcome, but worry whether the government will deliver on, with good reason. Cygnus Homes in Cambridgeshire build to the 'passive house' standard, engineered and insulated in such a way that just by living in the house it achieves a comfortable temperature, no extra heating required.

The energy bill for this house is about 75% less than the national average, and it can be built in less time by fewer workers than the traditional home. It shows that the construction industry can deliver the low carbon houses that Britain desperately needs, in very little time. So, why aren't we building them? Well because a couple of years ago in response to intense lobbying the government dropped something called the 'zero carbon home standard'.

As a result, housing developments with very efficient new homes like this one in Essex are the rarity rather than the norm. Even though innovative architects and developers say they can deliver them at a similar cost to more wasteful traditional homes.

So, the decision to scrap the zero carbon homes target, did that set everyone back do you think?

Tom Dollard: Undoubtedly yeah, it, um ... the industry had a clear target which was meant to be zero carbon homes at 2016 ... that was scrapped and ... and then there was a lot of confusion, there still is a lot of confusion, so ...

Reporter: So now there's an opportunity to put that back though, right?

Tom Dollard: Yeah, we need a clear target, um ... simple policy to set house builders and developers a standard for zero carbon homes or low carbon homes whatever it needs ... it just needs to be a standard.

Reporter: And you're saying in some ways it shows that it can be done, it's within our grasp, it's not impossible.

Tom Dollard: Exactly.

Commentator: Today's strategy includes most of the things needed to deliver a truly greener economy. But, say critics, this government mustn't repeat the mistakes of others by giving up on green measures that long-term benefit consumers and the environment.

UNIT 6

The power of the wind

Narrator: Wind power provides only about five percent of the world's energy needs today, but many environmental experts believe that figure could rise to almost 20% by 2030. Wind generates almost half a million megawatts of power—that's a 19% jump in just 5 years.

The UK is in a particularly good position to develop wind power because it is so, well, windy. At present, it ranks sixth in terms of capacity but is investing heavily in this renewable energy source. The percentage of electricity in the UK generated from wind power overtook that of coal, once Britain's primary source of energy, for the first time in 2016. The result was the lowest carbon emission rate since the 1920s.

The blades of the wind turbine turn a shaft, which passes the energy to a generator, which in turn transforms this energy into electricity. The wind is free, but the cost of power generation and storage actually makes wind power more expensive than traditional fossil fuel sources like coal, oil and gas. Smart technology is steadily bringing these costs down, however, and this trend is expected to continue.

There are two different types of wind power – onshore and offshore. Onshore wind farms are cheaper to build and maintain, but many people don't want windfarms in their areas. The turbines are quite noisy, and many people say they spoil the landscape.

Offshore windfarms, in contrast, are located in the sea, where few people care about their noise or appearance. The UK is a leader in offshore wind power. The London Array, off the east coast of England in the North Sea, is the largest offshore wind farm in the world.

The UK is also home to the world's first floating windfarm, off the northeast coast of Scotland.

Although there is considerable public support for wind power, there is also opposition to these large, noisy devices. It's also important to remember that all of them are subject to changes in weather patterns. There are windy days and not-so-windy days. There are also not-so-windy years. Denmark, a leader in wind power, saw its wind power level drop in 2016 because of a lack of wind. Nevertheless, the shift to renewable energy sources like wind is likely to continue unabated.

Energy analyst: If you look at a more flexible, more dynamic energy system, we're saying more electric vehicles on ... going out into the 2030s, then the backbone of that energy system should be cheap renewables. That is going to be the way to keep bills ... bills low and you won't find an energy analyst out there that disagrees with that vision of the future.

UNIT 7

Beijing Art Zone

Narrator: This was once a vast state-run military factory on the outskirts of Beijing, employing as many as 20,000 workers, complete with housing for the workers, athletic facilities, a hospital, and even its own orchestra. But that was the 1950s. Today, this factory complex presents a more peaceful and dramatically different face.

798 Art Zone became a space where artists could live and create art in a supportive community that included painters, sculptors, fashion designers, photographers and film directors. It attracted well known Chinese artists, such as Sui Jiangou, whose dinosaurs are popular with visitors.

Visitors stop to examine and photograph these Red Metal Men, not quite sure if they are singing, shouting, staring in surprise or just hoping to catch some raindrops!

Although the Art Zone began as a place for outsiders, artists whose work was not seen in traditional museums, it has become a part of the mainstream arts scene, a popular attraction with both local visitors and international tourists. The centre hosts art exhibitions, annual film festivals, fashion shows, art auctions and theatre productions, and it has all the services common to other tourist destinations, including gift shops and cafés like this one, located in an old train station that used to transport materials to and from the original factory. It's free to the public and tens of thousands of visitors enjoy the centre every day.

When it began, the 798 Art Zone provided inexpensive living and work space for struggling artists. Today the rents are high and only the most successful artists can afford to show their work here. The struggling artists have moved on to new locations – perhaps to the next 798.

UNIT 8

The retired men and women who love to walk

Commentator: Seventeen years ago, a group of newly retired men and women in Salford decided to meet up every week and go for a walk, once a week for seventeen years and today they're still going. The handful of original walkers has grown to fifty or so and they're loving it.

Wilma Harriman: When I go on a walk, I feel energized and I feel as if I can cope with things.

Mary Walker: My husband tried his best to get me swimming which I believe is the best form of exercise but um ... I'm frightened of the water.

Commentator: This group goes out for an hour at a time with two different routes for quicker and slower walkers, and it's precisely what health experts say all adults need to do, regular gentle exercise, even just ten minutes a day can help prevent cancer, heart disease and poor mental health.

Dr Jenny Harries: No fancy kit, no expensive gym memberships, sensible pair of shoes and off you go um ... and you can just err ... do it when you're taking the dog for a walk, do it if you're taking the kids to school, err ... do it if you're walking to work, so really easy but it really does have huge health benefits.

Commentator: Research by Public Health England suggests that we're taking less and less exercise, but people in the UK are 20% less active than in the 1960s. They say just a few minutes brisk walking every day could reverse that trend and would come with other benefits.

Barry Hazel: There are three benefits a) the exercise, b) the fresh air and c) the companionship and I think that's also very important because a lot of these people are widows or widowers and they might not see many people during the week.

Commentator: And these walkers say the other advantage of exercise is it makes the cup of tea afterwards taste even better.

ACKNOWLEDGEMENTS

The authors and publishers acknowledge the following sources of copyright material and are grateful for the permissions granted. While every effort has been made, it has not always been possible to identify the sources of all the material used, or to trace all copyright holders. If any omissions are brought to our notice, we will be happy to include the appropriate acknowledgements on reprinting and in the next update to the digital edition, as applicable.

Key: L = Left, R = Right, B = Below, C = Centre, T = Top.

Photo
All below images are sourced from Getty Images.

pp. 14–15: Pete Saloutos/Image Source; p. 19: © IKEA; p. 23: haoliang/E+; p. 31: sarayuth3390/iStock Editorial/Getty Images Plus; pp. 36–37: SIMON MAINA/AFP; p. 41: Barry Winiker/Photolibrary; p. 42: Rebecca Sapp/WireImage; p. 45 (L): Blend Images – Hill Street Studios/Brand X Pictures; p. 45 (R): Hero Images; pp. 58–59: Bloomberg; p. 62: Temmuzcan/iStock/Getty Images Plus; p. 64: Seksak Kerdkanno/EyeEm; p. 67: Eric Audras/ONOKY; p. 75: Hero Images; pp. 80–81: forrest9/iStock Editorial/Getty sImages Plus; p. 85 (levee): itasun/iStock/Getty Images Plus; p. 85 (tsunami): JIJI PRESS/AFP; p. 85 (dam): JOE KLAMAR/AFP; p. 85 (hurricane): Stocktrek Images; p. 85 (thames barrier): Andrew Holt/Photographer's Choice; p. 85 (flood): Matt Cardy/Getty Images News; p. 94 (wild fire): Andrew Korson/iStock/Getty Images Plus; p. 94 (dust strom): Pavliha/E+; pp. 102–103: Dillemma Photography/Moment; p. 108 (T): Christian Aslund/Lonely Planet Images; p. 108 (B): Anna Gorin/Moment; p. 111 (L): Barry Winiker/Photolibrary; p. 111 (R): Rick Gerharter/Lonely Planet Images; p. 113: George Rose/Getty Images News; pp. 124–125: ABDELHAK SENNA/AFP; p. 128 (photo 1): John Harper/Photodisc; p. 128 (photo 2): Universal Images Group; p. 128 (photo 3): Nenov/Moment; p. 128 (photo 4): FRED TANNEAU/AFP; p. 134 (T): Renate Frost/EyeEm; p. 134 (C): Carl Court/AFP; p. 134 (B): Hans-Peter Merten/The Image Bank; p. 142: shan.shihan/Moment; pp. 146–147: Tim E White/Photolibrary; p. 151 (a): AXEL SCHMIDT/DDP; p. 151 (b): Hannah Peters/Getty Images Entertainment; p. 151 (c): PETER PARKS/AFP; p. 151 (d): Niccolo Guasti/Getty Images Entertainment; p. 152: Jim Dyson/Getty Images News; p. 155: Henri Cartier-Bresson; p. 159 (T): lnzyx/iStock/Getty Images Plus; p. 159 (B): De Agostini Picture Library/De Agostini; p. 162: Ullstein bild; p. 163: Universal Images Group; pp. 168–169: Jed Share/Kaoru Share/Blend Images; p. 173: Klaus Tiedge/Blend Images; p. 175: Celia Peterson/arabianEye.

Front cover photography by Dillemma Photography/Moment

Video stills
All below stills are sourced from Getty Images.

p. 16, p. 60, p. 126 (video 1): Sky News/Film Image Partner; p. 38, p. 104, p. 126 (video 4), p. 170: ITN; p. 126 (video 2): Dorling Kindersley; p. 126 (video 3): Allstar Picture Library/Photolibrary Video; p. 148 (video 1, video 2, video 3): piggyfoto/Getty Images Editorial Footage; p. 148 (video 4): Zhang Peng/Getty Images Editorial Footage.

The following stills are sourced from BBC Worldwide Learning
p. 82: BBC Worldwide Learning.

Videos
All below clips are sourced from Getty Images and BBC Worldwide Learning.

Sky News/Film Image Partner; AFP Footage; SkyworksFootage/Creatas Video; ITN; nomagnolia/Creatas Video+/Getty Images Plus; Dorling Kindersley; Allstar Picture Library/ Photolibrary Video; Multi-bits/Image Bank Film; topnatthapon/Creatas Video; Multi-bits/Image Bank Film; Bloomberg Video - Footage/Bloomberg; Discovery FootageSource; Reel Entrepreneurs - Footage/Getty Images Editorial Footage; Multi-bits/Image Bank Film; topnatthapon/ Creatas Video; Spoonfilm/Moment Video RF; Kyodo News Video; Eddie Gerald; Video Journalist Africa – Footage; Zhang Peng/Getty Images Editorial Footage; piggyfoto; RPM Media Inc - Roberto & Christina Mitrotti/Image Bank Film; BBC Motion Gallery Editorial/BBC News; BBC Worldwide Learning.

Corpus
Development of this publication has made use of the Cambridge English Corpus (CEC). The CEC is a multi-billion word computer database of contemporary spoken and written English. It includes British English, American English and other varieties of English. It also includes the Cambridge Learner Corpus, developed in collaboration with the University of Cambridge ESOL Examinations. Cambridge University Press has built up the CEC to provide evidence about language use that helps to produce better language teaching materials.

Cambridge Dictionaries
Cambridge dictionaries are the world's most widely used dictionaries for learners of English. The dictionaries are available in print and online at dictionary.cambridge.org. Copyright © Cambridge University Press, reproduced with permission.

Typeset by emc design ltd.

UNLOCK SECOND EDITION ADVISORY PANEL

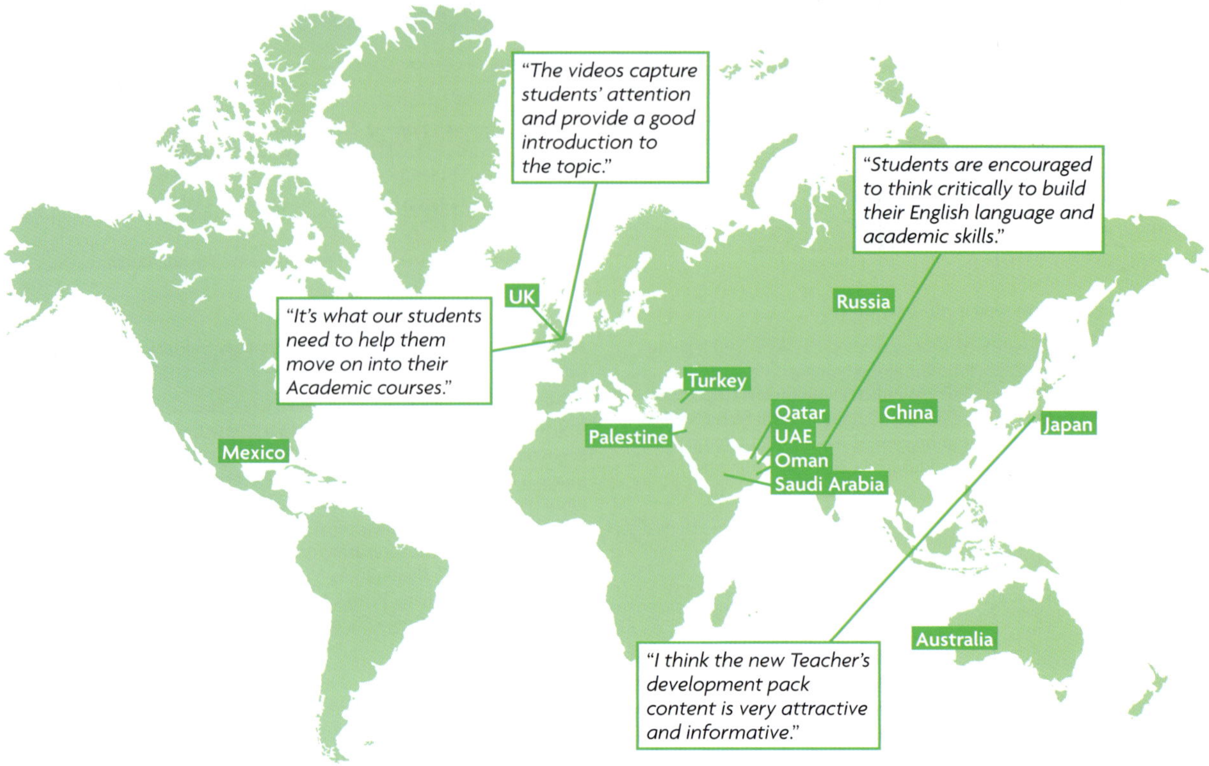

We would like to thank the following ELT professionals all around the world for their support, expertise and input throughout the development of *Unlock* Second Edition:

Adnan Abu Ayyash, Birzeit University, Palestine	Takayuki Hara, Kagoshima University, Japan	Megan Putney, Dhofar University, Oman
Bradley Adrain, University of Queensland, Australia	Esengül Hasdemir, Atilim University, Turkey	Wayne Rimmer, United Kingdom
Sarah Ali, Nottingham Trent International College (NTIC), United Kingdom	Irina Idilova, Moscow Institute of Physics and Technology, Russia	Sana Salam, TED University, Turkey
Ana Maria Astiazaran, Colegio Regis La Salle, Mexico	Meena Inguva, Sultan Qaboos University, Oman	Setenay Şekercioglu, Işık University, Turkey
Asmaa Awad, University of Sharjah, United Arab Emirates	Vasilios Konstantinidis, Prince Sultan University, Kingdom of Saudi Arabia	Robert B. Staehlin, Morioka University, Japan
Jesse Balanyk, Zayed University, United Arab Emirates	Andrew Leichsenring, Tamagawa University, Japan	Yizhi Tang, Xueersi English, TAL Group, China
Lenise Butler, Universidad del Valle de México, Mexico	Alexsandra Minic, Modern College of Business and Science, Oman	Valeria Thomson, Muscat College, Oman
Esin Çağlayan, Izmir University of Economics, Turkey	Daniel Newbury, Fuji University, Japan	Amira Traish, University of Sharjah, United Arab Emirates
Matthew Carey, Qatar University, Qatar	Güliz Özgürel, Yaşar University, Turkey	Poh Leng Wendelkin, INTO City, University of London, United Kingdom
Eileen Dickens, Universidad de las Américas, Mexico	Özlem Perks, Istanbul Ticaret University, Turkey	Yoee Yang, The Affiliated High School of SCNU, China
Mireille Bassam Farah, United Arab Emirates	Claudia Piccoli, Harmon Hall, Mexico	Rola Youhia, University of Adelaide College, Australia
Adriana Ghoul, Arab American University, Palestine	Tom Pritchard, University of Edinburgh, United Kingdom	Long Zhao, Xueersi English, TAL Group, China
Burçin Gönülsen, Işık University, Turkey		